MYSTIC
FIRE

Atulindra Nath Chaturvedi studied political science at Hindu College (Delhi University) and international studies at Jawaharlal Nehru University, Delhi. A media consultant and freelance writer, he has worked with *The Times of India*, *The Pioneer*, *Business Today* and *Tehelka*, and regularly contributed articles and book reviews for *Outlook*, *The Patriot* and *The Indian Express*.

Chaturvedi has to his credit several books, which include *Sri Aurobindo: Spiritual Revolutionary* (2002), *APJ Abdul Kalam: Scientist and Humanist* (2002), and *Dharma Gurus* (forthcoming). He has also annotated and written an introduction to *Hind Swaraj* by M.K. Gandhi (forthcoming).

MYSTIC FIRE

The Life of Sri Aurobindo

ATULINDRA NATH
CHATURVEDI

RUPA

Published by
Rupa Publications India Pvt. Ltd 2022
7/16, Ansari Road, Daryaganj
New Delhi 110002

Sales centres:
Allahabad Bengaluru Chennai
Hyderabad Jaipur Kathmandu
Kolkata Mumbai

ISBN: 978-93-5520-778-4

First impression 2022

10 9 8 7 6 5 4 3 2 1

The moral right of the author has been asserted.

Printed in India

Dedicated to the memory of my father
Triloki Nath Chaturvedi (1926–2020)
and my mother
Prakashvati Chaturvedi (1933–89)

You are my Lord, my Guru, my father,
and my mother.
Where can I go, leaving your lotus feet?
I am your child, though devoid of knowledge,
understanding and strength;
Pray keep this humble servant under your
shelter, O Lord.
—Tulsidas

And to
Dr Shruti Nada Poddar and Vedaaranya Haveli
and
Sujata Kohli and Raj Kutir

Contents

Long after this controversy is hushed in silence, long after this turmoil, this agitation ceases, long after he is dead and gone, he will be looked upon as the poet of patriotism, as the prophet of nationalism and the lover of humanity. Long after he is dead and gone, his words will be echoed and re-echoed not only in India, but across distant seas and lands. Therefore, I say that the man in his position is not only standing before the bar of this Court but before the bar of the High Court of History.

—Chittaranjan Das

Mr A.B. Clark, the Principal of the Baroda College, remarked to me, 'So you met Aurobindo Ghosh. Did you notice his eyes? There is mystic fire and light in them. They penetrate into the beyond.'

—Sir C.R. Reddy

The traditions of the past are very great in their own place, in the past, but I do not see why we should merely repeat them and not go farther. In the spiritual development of the consciousness upon earth the great past ought to be followed by a greater future.

—Sri Aurobindo

We of the coming day stand at the head of a new age of development...We do not belong to the past dawns, but to the noons of the future.

—Sri Aurobindo

There is no one who can write my biography nor is this the time to do it, supposing it has to be done at all. If the outward facts of the life are meant, anybody can do that and it has no importance— the best thing is to have some outsider to do that mess, if mess there must be.

—Sri Aurobindo

Preface
Why Sri Aurobindo?

This question was directed at me when I mentioned to an old friend that I was working on a book about Sri Aurobindo (Aurobindo Ghose) to mark his 150th birth anniversary. The answer is straightforward. Sri Aurobindo was a unique individual in the history of modern India. He was an individual who combined within himself the best of the East and the West. Born in India, educated in England, he became a pillar of the nationalist movement, in a political career that lasted for only three and a half years—with one full year spent in jail. He was the first person to call for the independence of India from British rule. His political writings make for fascinating reading even today. The strategies and tactics that he sponsored lead not only to the revolutionary groups that battled the British but also prepared the people of India for the Gandhian moment.

But Sri Aurobindo was more than just a freedom fighter and journalist. From the very beginning, he reached back in time to access India's ancient heritage—not to recreate it but to learn from it, revitalize it and make it relevant for the India of today and tomorrow. He was a poet, dramatist, philosopher, Sanskritist and literary critic. He foreshadowed Edward Said's theory of Orientalism a century earlier. At his ashram (a word he was not very comfortable with) in Pondicherry, he created a new kind of yoga—Integral Yoga. Sri Aurobindo was also one of the first internationalists after the two world wars.

The last major biography of Sri Aurobindo available in India was the majestic *Sri Aurobindo: A Biography and a History* by K.R. Srinivas Iyengar, which acquired its final shape in the third edition published in 1985. Since then, thanks to the diligent work of the Sri Aurobindo Ashram, much new documentation has appeared that helps us understand his life better. *The Complete Works of Sri Aurobindo*, in 36 volumes, has a huge mass of new material, primarily Sri Aurobindo's unpublished writings and information of a biographical nature. All this incredible wealth of material has been made use of in the making of this book.

Mystic Fire is a complete biography of Sri Aurobindo, but its specific focus is his involvement in the political life of India as a participant, and later, in Pondicherry, as an observer and occasional interventionist, publicly and privately. It is for this reason that a large part of the book relates to the pre-1910 years. An attempt has been made to dispel the myth that Sri Aurobindo in Pondicherry had completely turned his back on politics.

Aurobindo Ghose, in various spellings, is the name by which he was known before he went to Pondicherry. We shall call him Aurobindo, as that is the name by which he was known to his friends and foes alike—the surname was almost always not used, as if they were speaking of an intimate friend. By the 1930s and since then, he has been known as Sri Aurobndo, and that is how we shall address him in the years after 1910.

My thanks to Shri Matri Prasad, secretary, Sri Aurobindo Ashram, for his assistance. My thanks to the members of the Sri Aurobindo Ashram Archives, whose diligent work over the years is the bedrock of this book. Sri Aurobindo and The Mother would have been proud of them.

All photographs are courtesy Sri Aurobindo Ashram, Pondicherry. All quotations from the writings of Sri Aurobindo and The Mother, and from publications of the ashram are being used with the permission of the Sri Aurobindo Ashram Trust.

My thanks to Shri Manoj Das Gupta, Copyright Department, Sri Aurobindo Ashram Trust, for permission to quote from Sri Aurobindo's writings and other publications of the Ashram.

My thanks to the members of my family who regularly asked if the book had been finished, and if not, why? Their constant encouragement (read badgering) helped to motivate myself. Vidhu Khanna's comments, which she deemed to be witty, also had a role in the completion of the book. Thanks also to Naimuddin and Girish for keeping Softy Chaturvedi at bay, and for ensuring that I ate something daily.

R.K. Mehra had asked me some 20 years ago to write a small book on Sri Aurobindo, and encouraged me to continue writing—I am forever in his debt. Kapish Mehra is now carrying forward the rich legacy of Rupa with elan. Rudra Narayana Sharma and Upama Biswas have done a wonderful job on the production front. Amrita Chakravorty has also been very creative with the cover.

Mystic Fire is dedicated to the memory of my parents. The title comes from a conversation I had once had with my father, who asked what I would call such a book. He was interested when I explained the reasons, one of which is in the C.R. Reddy quote in the epigraph. The other was that a translation of Vedic hymns by Sri Aurobindo had the arresting title 'Hymns to the Mystic Fire'.

A few jottings made in late winter at Dr Shruti Nada Poddar's Vedaaranya Haveli in Ramgarh Shekhawati, Rajasthan, were the beginnings of *Mystic Fire*. The last words were written in Sujata Kohli's Raj Kutir in Ramgarh, Uttarakhand. I offer my thanks to both Shruti and Sujata for the opportunity to visit and experience the two Ramgarhs. Since the forts of the Righteous One frame *Mystic Fire*, it is only natural that it also be dedicated to Vedaaranya and Raj Kutir, and to Shruti and Sujata.

Atulindra Nath Chaturvedi
4 April 2022

Section I

The Poet of Patriotism

1

An Indian Childhood, an English Education (1872–93)

The British Empire was at its zenith in India in 1872. After the uprising of 1857 against increasing British domination had been crushed ruthlessly, the British Crown had taken over the reins of governance from the East India Company. Unique in the annals of history, the Company, although established for the purpose of trade in the Indian Ocean sea route, also conquered territory and ran a government in its colony. Its army outfought its trade rivals—the French, Dutch and Portuguese—and established British supremacy. Post 1857, this supremacy was further strengthened by the Crown through a system of direct (British India) and indirect rule (princely states). Administratively, the entire Indian subcontinent was under a single rule.

This led to the plunder of the Indian economy and its total subordination to British interests in a systematic manner, unlike the haphazard efforts of the Company. A network of railways connected the interior of the country to the coast, all the better to transport raw material to England to satisfy its commercial needs and deprive India of its wealth. Traditional Indian education was squeezed out, and schools and colleges were run on British lines. The intent was to create a class of people Indian in origin but English in every other way. They succeeded in this endeavour—a new middle class emerged—Indian, and fully conversant with the English language and cultural mores, believing that it was only the British who held India together, and that Indian culture was denigrate and inferior. Politically, this class had no means of expressing itself until the creation of the Indian National Congress in 1885 through the agency of a civil servant, Allan Octavian Hume, who, alarmed by the murmurs of unease he came across, sought to use the new organization to channelize discontent and defuse any tension against British rule.

It was this very class, ironically, which led the reaction to English claims of racial and cultural superiority. The lead was taken by Raja Rammohun Roy (born exactly a century before our protagonist) in Bengal. A social and religious reformer, he helped to found the Brahmo Samaj, a Hindu religious reform organization. It became quite influential, attracting the likes of Maharshi Debendranath Tagore, the father of the poet Rabindranath Tagore, and the mercurial Keshab Chandra Sen. Others began to explore India's ancient past and to reassert that its culture was inferior to none, and it was resilient enough to help chart the way to the future. This nascent cultural nationalism, endorsing India's past culture and taking pride in it, is collectively known as the Bengal Renaissance, and it laid the foundations for the political nationalism that arose in the last years of the nineteenth century.

Early Days in India

It was into this landscape of an arid political scenario and newly resurgent cultural activism that Aravinda Ackroyd Ghose was born—on 15 August 1872 in Calcutta. The newborn was given the unusual name Aravinda, which is the Sanskrit word for lotus, as his father wanted his third son to have a unique name. The middle name, Ackroyd, came from Annette Ackroyd, an English friend of Aurobindo's father (and the mother of William Beveridge, the father of the modern welfare state). Aurobindo spelt it as Akroyd, before dropping it altogether in 1893.

In a 1934 letter, Sri Aurobindo sardonically observed on his name:

> But look at the irony of human decisions and human hopes. My father who wanted all his sons to be great men—and succeeded in a small way with three of them—in a sudden inspiration gave me the name Aurobindo, till then not borne by anyone in India or the wide world, that I might stand out unique among the great by the unique glory of my name. And now look at the swarm of Aurobindos with their mighty deeds in England, Germany and elsewhere! Don't tell me it is my fault because of my indiscretion in becoming famous. When I went to the National College... my first public step towards the ignomies of fame, there was already an Aurobindo Prakash waiting for me there with the sardonic comments of the gods printed on his learned forehead.[1]

Aurobindo's maternal grandfather was Raj Narain Bose, who in his lifetime was acclaimed as the 'Grandfather of Indian Nationalism'. Raj Narain's father, Nanda Kishore Bose, was a clerk in the East India Company. Raj Narain proved to be a brilliant student, first at David Hare's school in Calcutta and then at Hindu College, Calcutta, which developed into Presidency College. Exposed to western rationalism, he lost faith in Hinduism and experimented with Islam and Christianity, and turned to meat and drink. As he wrote in his autobiography: 'While still a college student, several times I changed my religion:

---

[1] *Complete Works of Sri Aurobindo: Volume 35: Letters on Himself and the Ashram,* Sri Aurobindo Ashram, 1997, p. 8.

from Hindu to Unitarian Christian to Muslim to agnostic, all depending upon the influence of the book I was reading.'[2] The sudden deaths of both his father and wife stunned Raj Narain, and he finally found solace in Vedanta. He joined the Brahmo Samaj, and was, for some time, secretary to Rammohun Roy himself. He then went to Midnapore, where he became the headmaster of the government school, staying there until 1866. He became a propagandist for and a defender of Hinduism in the face of attacks on the religion by Christian missionaries. Sri Aurobindo once remembered, 'My grandfather started by being a Brahmo and ended by writing a book on Hinduism and proclaiming it as the best religion in the world.'[3] He started the Jatiya Mela, which, as the Jatiya Sabha, became a precursor of the Indian National Congress. He also started a revolutionary society of which the young Rabindranath Tagore was a member. He died in Deoghar in 1899.

Raj Narain's eldest daughter, the beautiful Swarnalata, married Dr Krishna Dhan Ghose, a Brahmo adherent and a strong-willed Anglophile civil surgeon in 1864. Born in Konnagar and orphaned at an early age, the impoverished boy, by dint of hard work, managed to study at the Calcutta Medical College. At the age of 21, he became a doctor in the Bengal government's service and was first posted at Bhagalpur (in present-day Bihar) and, later, at Rangpur and Khulna (in present-day Bangladesh). In Bhagalpur, he was an industrious propagator of Brahmo ideals.

After the birth of two sons—Benoybhushan and Manmohan—Krishna Dhan went for further medical studies to Aberdeen University in England in 1869. During his stay there, Krishna Dhan fell under the spell of English culture, which seemed to him

---

[2]Nahar, Sujata, *Mother's Chronicles Book Four: Mirra—Sri Aurobindo*, Mira Aditi Centre, 1995, p. 72.

[3]Purani, A.B., *Evening Talks with Sri Aurobindo*, Sri Aurobindo Ashram, 2001, p. 691.

to be the highest form of civilization. He proclaimed, 'We know the English are a superior race and can teach us much.'[4] He also came across the writings of Charles Darwin and his theory of evolution. Aurobindo later noted: 'Everyone makes all the forefathers of a great man very religious-minded, pious, etc. It is not true in my case at any rate. My father was a tremendous atheist.'[5]

When Krishna Dhan returned home in 1871, he had become a curious hybrid of the East and the West. He cut off all links with Konnagar when he was asked to undergo a ceremony of ritual purification, the superstitious custom required for someone who went overseas. Krishna Dhan instructed that the family was to speak in English only—no Indian language was to be spoken. The young children managed to pick up rudimentary Hindustani from servants but no Bengali or any other Indian language. Swarnalata had to wear European dress only, as did the children. But this did not detract from his love of Bengali culture, and, in Rangpur, he came to be known as Suez Canal, the link between the English and the Bengalis. Krishna Dhan's Brahmo affiliation also withered, to the distress of Raj Narain.

We have no information about Aurobindo's childhood except an anecdote about a visit from his maternal uncle, Jogendra Bose. Jogendra held a mirror to Aurobindo, and pointing at the image, said 'See, monkey!' Aurobindo took the mirror, and pointing at Jogendra's image, exclaimed, 'See, big monkey!'

Krishna Dhan then took the three brothers to Darjeeling, where he entered them at the Loreto Convent, run by Irish nuns, for their first formal schooling. Intended for the children of English officials, the medium of instruction was English, and the convent was run on the lines of an English school.

[4]Nahar, Sujata, and Michel Danino, *Aurobindo and Mother to Prithwi Singh*, Mira Aditi, 1998, p. 30.
[5]Purani, A.B., *Evening Talks with Sri Aurobindo*, Sri Aurobindo Ashram, 2007, p. 691.

A visit by Annette Ackroyd gives us another glimpse of the young Aurobindo: 'The little fellow had a grey suit, very becoming—and is greatly aged—grown tall and boyish. I was struck particularly by the broadening of his forehead. He was pleased to see me, I think but all were quite silent except for an extorted yes! Or no!'[6]

But Krishna Dhan was still not satisfied with placing his children in an alien environment in India. He went a step further and decided to take them to another alien environment—this time, in an alien land—England. But before he took them from Darjeeling, a strange incident took place. In 1926, Sri Aurobindo recalled:

> I was lying down one day when I saw suddenly a great Tamas [darkness] rushing into me and enveloping me and the whole universe. After that I had a great darkness always hanging on to me all through my stay in England. I believe that darkness had something to do with the Tamas that came upon me. It left me only when I was coming back to India.[7]

Life in England

In mid-1879, Krishna Dhan and his entire family—to which a young daughter, Sarojini, had been added—left for England. Krishna Dhan had struck up a friendship in India with Edward Glazier, the collector of Rangpur. Glazier had a cousin in Manchester, the clergyman William Drewett, with whom the boys could be left while Krishna Dhan sought medical help for Swarnalata, who had shown increasing signs of mental instability. Swarnalata was, by then, heavily pregnant, and a boy was born

---

[6]Heehs, Peter, *The Lives of Sri Aurobindo*, Columbia University Press, 2008, p. 26.
[7]Purani, A.B., *Evening Talks with Sri Aurobindo*, Sri Aurobindo Ashram, 2007, p. 393.

later in England. He was named Emaneul Matthew Ghose, but later had it changed to Barindra Kumar Ghose or Barin. He would play a key role in elder brother Aurobindo's revolutionary career. Before embarking for England, Krishna Dhan had a photograph of the entire family taken at a studio. In the photograph, everyone can be seen wearing European clothes, and a young Aurobindo looks out quietly and steadily at the world—a look that was never to change (at least in photographs).

Since the period for which he had taken leave was short, Krishna Dhan had to turn back almost immediately after arrival. He quickly arranged medical treatment for Swarnalata in London, after which she returned to India with the two younger children, her health having seemingly improved. Krishna Dhan left his three sons with Drewett in Manchester, and promised to send £360 every year. He also left strict instructions that they were to be totally isolated from anything to do with India, Indians, Indian religion or Indian culture. When asked about their religious upbringing, Krishna Dhan left it to the children to decide for themselves when they reached an appropriate age. Interestingly, in 1934, almost identical advice was given by Sri Aurobindo to Prithwi Singh about his children: 'Most of them are too young to have an intelligent will in such matters as yet and in a matter like sadhna there should be no pressure or influence of any kind. The delay will give some of them time to grow towards a possibility of a clear and willed choice.'[8] Krishna Dhan then sailed back to India and his job. He was destined never to see his three elder children again.

Manchester was far removed from the world of India, from the warmth of Bengal and the natural beauty of Darjeeling. The city was at the heart of the Industrial Revolution sweeping through the western world at the time, and with cotton manufacture at its core, it was the world's first industrial city. For the elder

---

[8]Danino & Nahar, p. 30.

boys, it would have been a trying time. For a child as young as Aurobindo, it must have been an especially traumatic experience. An anguished letter that Manmohan wrote to an English friend, the poet Laruence Binyon, in 1888, probably expresses the despair of the brothers at this sudden abandonment and the lack of family life and parental love:

> All childhood and boyhood is expansive. This human ivy stretches passionately forth its young tendrils, and the warm feelings are at the forefront, yearning to bestow and to be reciprocated: it is all heart; its brain lies undeveloped. It is the wise forethought of Nature that this should be so; but, in my case, Fate came between and cancelled her decrees; and, what to others is the bright portion of their life, its heaven and refuge, was for me bitterly and hopelessly blighted. You will not understand me, unless I tell a circumstance of my life which is unhappily both painful for me to reveal, and for you to hear. I had no mother. She is insane. You may judge the horror of this, how I strove to snatch a fearful love, but only succeeded in hating and loathing, and at last becoming cold. My father was kind but stern, and I never saw much of him.[9]

Aurobindo remembered the early Manchester days in an undated, incomplete note, 'I myself had when a boy of 8 or 9 a vivid dream which I never forgot of myself alone in my bed—I used to be sent to bed much earlier than my brothers—and lay there in a sort of constant terror of the darkness and phantoms and burglars till my brothers came up...'[10] This may have been the outcome of his loneliness. In another instance, Aurobindo stunned his

[9]Purani, A.B., *The Life of Sri Aurobindo*, Sri Aurobindo Ashram, 1978, p. 24.
[10]*Complete Works of Sri Aurobindo: Volume 35: Letters on Himself and the Ashram*, Sri Aurobindo Ashram, 1997, p. 9.

listeners with this self-assessment of himself at this time: 'I was a great coward virtually and I was weak physically and could not do anything. Only my will was strong. Nobody could have imagined that I could face the gallows or carry on a revolutionary movement.'[11] Aurobindo, being of a young age, was educated at home, while his brothers went to Manchester Grammar School. Drewett, who had studied at Oxford, taught him Latin and English history, while his wife taught the young boy French, geography and mathematics. Aurobindo later averred that he did not learn any science either at the Drewetts' or later at school.

A rumour arose in later years that Aurobindo had converted to Christianity, probably because of his Christian middle name. When Sri Aurobindo was told about it, he said that he had once been present at a meeting of non-conformists during a visit to Cumberland in North-West England. He had been taken there by the landlady of the house that he was staying in. After the meeting finished, a priest had come over, asked some questions, to which he had received no reply, and everyone present had suddenly shouted, 'He is saved!' Asked to say a prayer, the nonplussed boy had done so. He never attended church, nor was he ever attracted by Christianity. But the Bible and Christianity were the only scriptures and religion that he was aware of before his return to India.

At first, letters and the remittances from Krishna Dhan to Drewett arrived regularly, which suddenly became infrequent and finally stopped. Krishna Dhan's life had undergone a drastic change after his return home. At first, Swarnalata had seemed to have recovered, but soon her erratic behaviour recurred, to the point that Krishna Dhan could no longer tolerate it. He finally made arrangements for her stay in nearby Rohini, with Sarojini and Barin. Soon after, he was forced to remove both children from

---

[11]Purani, A.B., *Evening Talks with Sri Aurobindo*, Sri Aurobindo Ashram, 2007, p. 394.

Rohini, by virtually kidnapping them, and send them to the house of a friend in Calcutta. At work also, Krishna Dhan's position underwent a radical change. A new district magistrate had arrived at Khulna. He found that Krishna Dhan had a role to play in almost everything in the district. Irritated, he decided to sideline him. The stunned Krishna Dhan, till then an Anglophile, became embittered. This clearly was not the fair play that the English prided themselves on. The cost of maintaining two households combined with his charitable largesse made a considerable dent in his finances. The result was financial pressure on the three boys in England.

Drewett quit his job and migrated to Australia. During a halt in Calcutta, he somehow managed to get his arrears from Krishna Dhan. Back in England, the three boys were now in the charge of Drewett's mother, having moved to London. A pious, dyed-in-the-wool Christian, she did her best to convert the brothers to her faith. As the tension between them rose, matters came to a head when Manmohan made an injudicious remark about Moses. Old Mrs Drewett stormed out, saying that she could not live in the same house as unbelievers. While relieved at her departure, it also meant that the brothers were now completely on their own. They had to move out of the flat at Shepherds Bush that they lived in and take lodgings elsewhere. This was at Cromwell Road, where the South Kensington Liberal Club had its headquarters. The secretary was James Cotton, the brother of Henry Cotton, an old India hand. James was to play a crucial role in a pivotal moment in Aurobindo's life just a few years later. To make ends meet, Benoybhushan worked at the club for a low salary.

What were they doing in London? Manmohan and Aurobindo had been admitted to London's St. Paul's, one of the foremost schools in the country, in 1884. Aurobindo's proficiency in Latin, thanks to Drewett, was now matched by an equally sound knowledge of Greek, taught by D.F. Walker, the headmaster of St. Paul's. Aurobindo's obvious intelligence, knowledge and ability ensured that he rose rapidly through the different classes. However, by the time he reached Class Upper VIII in 1887, the teachers' report complained of laziness. Sri Aurobindo admitted that schoolwork did not take up much of his time, as he 'was already at ease in them and did not think it necessary to labour over them any longer.'[12] He, instead, focused on reading outside the curriculum—English and French poetry, fiction and history. Nevertheless, despite his lack of academic diligence, he still managed to win the Bedford Prize in history, and, in 1889, the second prize in the Butterworth Prize for knowledge of English literature.

Aurobindo, while accepted by his schoolfellows as brilliant, did not have any intimate friends among them, partly because of his aversion to sports of any kind. Moreover, his interests were clearly intellectual. He took part in the school's English and French debating societies, and spoke on Jonathan Swift and John Milton when the literary society was formed. He had already written some poetry, which had been published in *Fox's Weekly* during the Manchester days, but now took it more seriously, having been encouraged by Laurence Binyon's positive reaction to some of his efforts. Of these poems, which were later published in India, Sri Aurobindo noted, 'What these poems express is the education and imaginations and ideas and feelings created by a purely European culture and surroundings—it could not be otherwise.'[13] Percy Bysshe Shelley was his favourite poet at the time, with 'The Revolt of Islam' being read over and over. The poems that Aurobindo wrote during this time, along with a few others written in India, were privately published in India in 1898 as *Songs of Myrtilla*.

---

[12]*Complete Works of Sri Aurobindo: Volume 36: Autobiographical Notes and Other Writings of Historical Interest*, Sri Aurobindo Ashram, 1997, p. 28.
[13]Ibid. 29.

They were heavily influenced by the Romantic movement, and there is little evidence of the originality of the poet that was soon to emerge, far less the creator of the epic *Savitri*.

The brothers used to take long holiday walks, an escape from the schoolwork and the hardships that they had to face in everyday life. We learn from the letters that Manmohan wrote to Binyon that they frequented places such as Keswick, Derbyshire and Hastings. Aurobindo remembered: 'During a whole year a slice or two of sandwich bread and butter and a cup of tea in the morning and evening a penny saveloy formed the only food.'[14] A poor diet had led to physical weakness in all the three brothers, and their worn faces and shabby clothes were noticed at school.

The ambition of Krishna Dhan, the very purpose of their exile, had been for the three brothers to be educated in such a way that they would be able to sit for the Indian Civil Service (ICS) examinations, which were held only in England at Cambridge University. Benoybhushan's abilities were not up to the mark, Manmohan had embarked on the life of a writer, so that left Aurobindo to fulfil his father's ambitions. But the financial situation dictated that Aurobindo win a scholarship if he were to study at Cambridge and for the ICS simultaneously. It was with this aim that Aurobindo put his nose to the grind in his last year at St. Paul's, showing a sharp improvement in his marks.

Cambridge

The hard work paid off. Aurobindo sat for the King's College scholarship examination in December 1889 and stood first. He was informed by Oscar Browning, a well-known scholar, that his

---

[14]*Sri Aurobindo Birth Centenary Library*, Volume 26, Sri Aurobindo Ashram, 1970–73, p. 2.

papers were 'the best he had ever seen and quite remarkable'.[15] He then sat for the gruelling 13-day ICS examination the following June. The curriculum was heavily tilted in favour of those who had studied in England, especially Greek and Latin. Aurobindo stood eleventh out of 250 candidates. In Greek, he got 557 out of 600, and stood second in Latin. He scored highly in all the other papers too. In short, Aurobindo's performance was a double triumph. Not only had he bested the English at Cambridge, he had also bested them in the ICS examinations in the very subjects that were like Achilles heel for Indian candidates. Thus was born the legend of Aurobindo.

Sri Aurobindo was to remember his Cambridge years wistfully: 'I think there is no student of Oxford or Cambridge who does not look back in after days on the few years of his undergraduate life as, of all the scenes he has moved in, that which calls up the happiest memories.'[16] It is an interesting comment, given the heavy workload that he was now called upon to take up—under the terms of the scholarship, he had to take the complete Classics course and sit for the Tripos examination. Though the courses were similar to what he had been taught at St. Paul's, the workload and time taken for classes were back-breaking. Add to this the fact of the ICS course—general jurisprudence, law of evidence, Hindu and Muslim codes, civil and criminal procedure of British India, Indian history and political economy. He also had to learn Bengali—from R.M. Towers, an Englishman whose command of the language was indifferent. Incredibly, Aurobindo managed to learn Sanskrit on his own—'I learnt Sanskrit by reading the Naladamayani episode in the Mahabharat...with minute care several times.'[17]

[15]*Complete Works of Sri Aurobindo: Volume 36: Autobiographical Notes and Other Writings of Historical Interest*, Sri Aurobindo Ashram, 1997, p. 122.

[16]*Complete Works of Sri Aurobindo: Volume 1: Early Cultural Writings*, Sri Aurobindo Ashram, 1997, p. 353.

[17]*Complete Works of Sri Aurobindo: Volume 35: Letters on Himself and the Ashram*,

Interestingly, in the ICS examination, Aurobindo bested a certain Charles Beachcroft, pushing him into second place in Greek. Beachcroft had his revenge. He, in turn, beat Aurobindo into second place—in Bengali! Friendly acquaintances at Cambridge, their paths would cross again in the years to come, in a manner and situation no one could have predicted.

Aurobindo's formidable workload and his efforts were put into perspective by G.W. Prothero, a historian who came to know him well, in a letter to James Cotton:

> He performed his part of the bargain, as regards the College, most honourably, and took a high place in the 1st class of the classical Tripos at the end of the second year of his residence. He also obtained certain college prizes, showing command of English and literary ability. That a man should have been able to do this (which alone is quite enough for most undergraduates) and at the same time too keep up with his ICS works, proves very unusual industry and capacity. Besides his classical scholarship he possessed a knowledge of English literature far beyond the average of undergraduates, and wrote a much better English style than most young Englishmen. Moreover, the man has not only ability but character.[18]

It was imperative for Aurobindo not to flounder, in either stream, for financial reasons. The scholarship brought in £80, and the ICS stipend, £300. This money was used to fund Aurobindo's life in Cambridge as well as that of his brothers. Krishna Dhan, on learning of the scholarship, had stopped sending money. The reserved almost shy youth made as few friends at Cambridge as he had at St. Paul's—the most notable of whom was Keshav Ganesh

---

Sri Aurobindo Ashram, 1997, p. 12.
[18]Purani, A.B., *The Life of Sri Aurobindo*, Sri Aurobindo Ashram, 1978, p. 20.

Deshpande, who was at St. John's at Cambridge, along with a few Irishmen. He also struck up a friendship with an Indian student in London—Chittaranjan Das, who was prevented from joining the ICS due to his political activities.

While Manmohan was vocal about his political opinions, which were quite radical in nature, Aurobindo kept to himself. But his understanding of the impact of British rule in India was hardening, thanks partly to the newspaper cuttings that his father had started to send, listing the cruelties perpetrated against Indians. Krishna Dhan was now denouncing the British in his letters as unjust. Sri Aurobindo commented on an early biography: 'At the age of eleven Sri Aurobindo had already received strongly the impression that a period of general upheaval and great revolutionary changes was coming in the world and he himself was destined to play a part in it. His attention was now drawn to India and this feeling was soon canalised into the idea of the liberation of his own country.'[19]

Aurobindo joined the newly created Indian Majlis at Cambridge, an association of Indian students, and, for some time, was its secretary. Sri Aurobindo later said that he had delivered 'revolutionary speeches' at the Majlis, but we have no record of its proceedings. However, a few fragmentary notes written during this time have come to light, which may have been related to the Majlis. In the longest note, he wrote,

> The patriot who passes judgement on a great movement in an era of change and turmoil, should be very confident that he has something worth saying before he ventures to speak; but if he can really put some new aspect on a momentous question or emphasise any side of it that has not been clearly understood, it (is) his bounden duty to ventilate (it).

---

[19]*Complete Works of Sri Aurobindo: Volume 36: Autobiographical Notes and Other Writings of Historical Interest*, Sri Aurobindo Ashram, 1997, p. 31.

Another says, 'It is time that an Indian who has devoted his best thoughts and aspirations to the service of his country, should have in turn a patient hearing...' And there is the ominous 'India is indeed a snake who has rejected her outworn winter weeds...'[20] Nothing earth-shaking in these words, but they were a clear portent of what was to come in just a few years, both in terms of thought and expression.

Among the poems he wrote at the time is one on Charles Stewart Parnell, the Irish leader, after his death. The poem has been taken to indicate the influence of Parnell, but Sri Aurobindo denied that Parnell had any impact on his thinking. Aurobindo also joined a revolutionary society shortly before his departure for India called the Lotus and Dagger. Along with his brothers, he took a vow to work towards the liberation of India. However, it does not seem to have flourished. Sri Aurobindo's disciple and biographer Ambulal Purani's assessment of the Majlis period is close to the mark: 'Sri Aurobindo's advocacy of Indian political freedom in the Majlis at Cambridge was not the unripe eloquence of a raw undergraduate. It was something that comes from a deep conviction of the soul. That this was so is amply borne out by the fact of his plunging into Indian politics immediately on his return to India.'[21]

Having cleared the final ICS examination, Aurobindo now had time for his favourite pastime—reading. For the first time, he came into contact with Indian philosophy through an ICS note on the six systems of Indian philosophy. Sri Aurobindo later wrote, 'The basic idea of the Self caught me when I was in England. I tried to realise what the Self might be. The first Indian writings that took hold of me were the Upanishads and these raised in me a strong

[20]*Complete Works of Sri Aurobindo: Volume 6: Bande Mataram — I–II*, Sri Aurobindo Ashram, 1997, p. 3.

[21]Purani, A.B., *The Life of Sri Aurobindo*, Sri Aurobindo Ashram, 1978, p. 342.

enthusiasm and I tried to translate them.'[22] Aurobindo tried to read them in the original Sanskrit but found that his knowledge of the language was not yet up to the task, and instead turned to the translations by Max Mueller. Around this time, Aurobindo also had his first spiritual experience, though he did not quite understand what it was until later. Thus, almost towards the end of his stay in England, a lifelong quest began.

Aurobindo may have passed the ICS examination, but he had one last hurdle to cross—horse riding. He failed to cross that hurdle. This was to become one of the two most celebrated and debated events in the life of Aurobindo, along with his sudden departure from the political field. What happened? We can piece together the sequence of events from contemporary documents and Aurobindo's own comments over the years. According to Sri Aurobindo, his interest in the ICS had begun to fade, but he was reluctant to face his father with the fact. 'I appeared for the ICS because my father wanted it and I was too young to understand. Later I found out what sort of work it is and I had a disgust for administrative life and I had no interest in administrative work. My interest was in poetry and literature and study of language and patriotic action.'[23] The decline in Aurobindo's enthusiasm is borne out by his marks. After having stood eleventh in the entrance, he claimed the twenty-third position in a class of 46 in the first periodic examination in 1891. He improved his position to nineteenth in the second periodic examination. In the final examination, he just about scraped through, ranking thirty-seventh out of 44 candidates. In Sanskrit, he was in the bottom half, and in Bengali, he was second last. By this time, Krishna Dhan, through the good offices of Henry Cotton, had

---

[22]*Complete Works of Sri Aurobindo: Volume 36: Autobiographical Notes and Other Writings of Historical Interest*, Sri Aurobindo Ashram, 1997, p. 113.
[23]Purani, A.B., *The Life of Sri Aurobindo*, Sri Aurobindo Ashram, 1978, p. 27.

ensured that Aurobindo would get a prestigious posting in the district of Arrah.

Aurobindo had a medical issue, which was soon resolved to the satisfaction of the authorities. However, he failed the riding test not once but twice. He was given several opportunities to repeat the test but failed to turn up at the appointed time. He was given a final try at Woolwich, where he deliberately arrived late. The instructor had already left. As a result, Aurobindo was informed on 17 November 1892 that he had been rejected and would not become a member of the ICS. Sri Aurobindo later noted, 'He felt no call for the ICS and was seeking some way to escape from the bondage. By certain manouevers he managed to get himself disqualified for riding without himself rejecting the service, which his family would not have allowed him to do.'[24] A few years later, Aurobindo said in an interview: 'If I was not actually glad, I was certainly not disappointed because the civil service was barred to me. I have never been fond of constraint of any sort and I was really not sorry to forego the service.'[25]

At this point, James Cotton swung into action, prodded by Prothero. He appears to have made Aurobindo write a letter to Lord Kimberley, the secretary of state, appealing to be given another chance. Cotton added a recommendation of his own and also Prothero's letter quoted earlier. The appeal went up and down the bureaucratic chain but to no avail. The commissioners of the ICS refused to agree to the appeal. The matter finally landed back on the table of Kimberley, who rejected it out of hand. He noted that it was necessary for anyone serving in India to be able to ride, and anyway 'I should much doubt whether Mr Ghose would be a desirable addition to the service...'[26] Aurobindo believed that

[24]Ibid. 31.

[25]Interview in *Empire*, 8 May 1909, republished in *Bengalee*, 9 May 1909. Cited in: Heehs, Peter, *The Lives of Sri Aurobindo*, Columbia University Press, 2008, p. 32.

[26]Purani, A.B., *The Life of Sri Aurobindo*, Sri Aurobindo Ashram, 1978, p. 346.

information about his involvement with the Majlis had been shared with the authorities, and that it was the final nail in the ICS coffin. Nevertheless, it was agreed that Aurobindo would be paid the remainder of his ICS stipend, as he had passed the examination. This took off a little of the pressure on his finances.

What was to be done now? Once again, James Cotton stepped into the breach. Maharaja Sayajirao Gaekwad of Baroda was on a visit to London. Cotton was able to arrange an interview for Aurobindo with the Maharaja. The interview went well, and Aurobindo was offered a job in the Baroda State Service. He accepted the offer of a pay of ₹200, which was considered cheap for an 'ICS man'. Aurobindo may not have been amoured of being a civil servant in British India, but he probably thought the conditions would be better in an Indian princely state. Finances dictated that Aurobindo return to India as early as possible. This meant that he did not get his degree, as it would have required another year at Cambridge. He might have got the degree, given his academic performance, if he had made a request, but he did not do so, as he believed that such a degree would have been useful only if he intended to pursue an academic career.

Meanwhile, Krishna Dhan had no idea at all of the dramatic events that were unfolding in England, dashing all his hopes and plans. He had written with great pride about his three sons, and specifically of Aurobindo, to his brother-in-law Jogendra Bose in 1890: 'Ara, I hope will yet glorify his country by a brilliant administration. I shall not live to see it, but remember this letter if you do.'[27]

Krishna Dhan tried to find out when Aurobindo would return to India, under the impression that he would be joining the ICS. The evidence is scanty as to the course of events. But it appears that in September 1892 he travelled to Bombay to get

---

[27]Ibid. 21.

information on Aurobindo's arrival but failed to do so. He returned to Bengal depressed. He received a telegram from Grindlay's, his bank, the incorrect information that Aurobindo had been on the *Roumania*, which sank off Lisbon on 27 October. Thinking his son dead, Krishna Dhan's health spiraled into decline, and he died alone, probably on 14 December 1892, murmuring the name of Aurobindo. Aurobindo learnt of the death of Krishna Dhan some time before his departure for India. The only comment he later made on Krishna Dhan's untimely death was that his father must have loved him, as his was the name on his lips as he died.

Going Home

Aurobindo left England on 11 January 1893 on the ship *Carthage*. He left England after having lived there for 14 years, and with no regrets whatsoever. As Sri Aurobindo later noted, 'There was no...regret in leaving England, no attachment to the past or misgivings for the future. Few friendships were made in England and none were very intimate; the mental atmosphere was not found congenial.' Furthermore, 'There was an attachment to English and European thought and literature, but not to England; he had no ties there...'[28] Aurobindo was completely and totally indifferent to the English and may have actually hated them. It was not England but France, which he never visited, with which he felt some affinity. Aurobindo never returned to England.

A few years later, Aurobindo wrote a poem titled 'L'envoie', which captures his seamless transition from West to East, with the imagery moving from Greece to Italy, until it finally reaches India:

> *For in Sicilian olive-groves no more*
> *Or seldom must my footprints now be seen,*

---

[28]*Complete Works of Sri Aurobindo: Volume 36: Autobiographical Notes and Other Writings of Historical Interest*, Sri Aurobindo Ashram, 1997, p. 35.

Nor tread Athenian lanes, nor yet explore
Parnassus or thy voiceful shores, O Hippocrene.
Me from her lotus heave Saraswati
Has called to regions of eternal snow
And Ganges pacing to the southern sea,
Ganges upon whose shores the flower of Eden blow.[29]

Aurobindo landed at Apollo Bunder in Bombay on 6 February 1893. When he had left India, a great darkness had descended on him. As he approached India, it seemed to disappear. When he set foot again on Indian soil, he felt 'a vast calm...; this calm surrounded him and remained for long months afterwards...' Sri Aurobindo explained: 'When I landed in Bombay a great calm and quiet descended upon me. Then there was the experience of the Self, the Purusha.'[30] There was no one waiting for him at the dock. He reached the Bombay railway station and caught the train to Baroda, where the Maharaja was waiting for him.

---

[29]*The Complete Works of Sri Aurobindo: Volume 2: Collected Poems*, Sri Aurobindo Ashram, 1997, p. 37.
[30]Purani, A.B., *Evening Talks with Sri Aurobindo*, Sri Aurobindo Ashram, 2007, p. 612.

2

Roots of Revolution in Baroda (1893–1906)

Baroda in the late nineteenth century was one of the relatively better-off princely states of British India. The state, in some ways, was socially and economically progressive, as compared to the rest of British India. This was thanks to Sayajirao Gaekwad III, who had been adopted in 1875 after the last ruler had died without a male issue. Sayajirao ascended to the throne in 1881.

He immediately instituted a slew of wide-ranging reforms— universal primary education, a ban on child marriage, removal of untouchability, a law for divorce as well as encouragement of the fine arts. In the economic sphere, he encouraged the textile industry and founded the State Bank of Baroda, which existed until recent years. He expanded Baroda's narrow-gauge railway network, which still exists. A water reservoir was dug at Ajwa, which supplies water to Baroda even today. Always on the lookout for talented people to help run the state, it is not surprising that Sayajirao hired someone as young and unproven but promising as Aurobindo. Little did he know what he was letting himself in for.

Civil Servant

Aurobindo's first posting in the Baroda administration was as an attaché or probationer at the settlement department, according to the first documentary record available of his service in Baroda, dated 18 February 1893. It adds that his salary of ₹200 was to commence from 8 February, which would be the day that he joined service. It further added that Aurobindo should learn Gujarati, the official language of the state, within a period of six months. Sri Aurobindo recalled, 'I was put at first in the Settlement Department, not on any post, but for learning work.'[31] Aurobindo did not initially take the language requirements seriously, even after being warned of a pay cut. He finally learnt both Gujarati and Marathi, which eventually brought the tally of languages that he knew to 12—English, Greek, Latin, French, German, Spanish, Italian, Sanskrit, Bengali, Gujarati, Marathi and Hindi. Later, he added one more in Pondicherry—Tamil.

A year later, he was moved to the revenue department, again as a probationer. But the Maharaja had not forgotten his cut-price ICS man. In May 1895, Aurobindo was summoned by the Maharaja to Ootacamund (popularly known as Ooty) in South India. The Maharaja was vacationing there, having just returned from Europe. A scandal had arisen in the revenue department, and protests had taken place in Baroda against the state's land policy in 1894–95. At the centre of the controversy was V.S. Bapat, an officer in the department who had been indicted by the courts. The Maharaja wanted Aurobindo to write a summary of the entire affair for his understanding.

Aurobindo immediately ran into trouble while travelling on his first official tour. From Bombay, he sent a telegram to his

---

[31]*Complete Works of Sri Aurobindo: Volume 36: Autobiographical Notes and Other Writings of Historical Interest*, Sri Aurobindo Ashram, 1997, p. 40.

superior officer that he needed an intelligent peon, and to send one immediately. His superior fired back he could hire one in Bombay if he so wanted. Aurobindo decided to do without one, and made it unscathed to Ooty. The Maharaja was obviously pleased with the work that he did, for on return to Baroda, Aurobindo found himself richer by Rs. 50, his salary having been increased by that amount. The state's diwan or prime minister was also told to give Aurobindo some responsible work.

The Maharaja then began to call Aurobindo over to the palace, unofficially, for work, which included drafting letters and reports. Towards the end of 1895, he was transferred to the diwan's office, and stayed there till 1898. He would have to draft letters in English addressed to British officials, amongst other tasks. Even during the period when he was teaching at Baroda College, Aurobindo would be called by the Maharaja for some work or the other. Once, in 1901, he was asked to teach the Maharaja's children in the absence of their regular tutor. He thought them dull, and one of them, Indira, the Maharaja's only daughter and later the maharani of Cooch-Behar, told Karan Singh her memories of Aurobindo the tutor: 'She remembered that Sri Aurobindo used to come to teach her and her brothers, and recalls that they used often to play truant because he was too immersed in thoughts and idealistic dreaming really to pay much attention to them.'[32] At this time, he was ordered to prepare a report on 20 years of state administration. Despite numerous reminders, he studiously ignored his orders and never wrote the reports. On occasion, Aurobindo was asked to do tasks that could have been attended to by anyone else. For instance, he once was asked to prepare the Maharaja's travel plans in Europe after consulting the appropriate railway timetables. The Maharaja once also asked

---

[32]Singh, Karan, *Prophet of Indian Nationalism: A Study of the Political Thought of Sri Aurobindo Ghosh 1893–1910*, G. Allen and Unwin, 1963, p. 47.

Aurobindo to help him improve his English through examples of strict application of the rules of grammar!

G.S. Sardesai, a fellow officer and later a well-known historian, remembered:

> Once the Maharaja had to address a social conference. Sri Aurobindo prepared the speech. The Maharaja, after hearing it, said: 'Can you not, Arabind Babu, tone it down? It is too fine to be mine.' Sri Aurobindo replied smiling: 'Why make a change for nothing? Do you think, Maharaja, that if it is toned down a little, people will believe it to be yours? Good or bad, whatever it be, people will always say that the Maharaja always gets his lectures written by others. The main thing is that the thoughts are yours.'[33]

A report and a speech that Aurobindo wrote during this period stand out. The report on trade in 1902 prepared for the Maharaja and the speech at the industrial exhibition at Ahmedabad the same year will be discussed in detail for the light they shed on Aurobindo's own economic thinking at this time.

The Maharaja once took Aurobindo to Kashmir as his secretary in 1903. The experiment was never repeated, as there was much friction between them. What happened? Apparently, Aurobindo did not turn up when summoned by the Maharaja, twice. The incensed Maharaja went to Aurobindo's room to roust him out— only to find him asleep. The Maharaja quietly went away, leaving his secretary to sleep in peace. Barin recalled a similar incident in Baroda:

> One morning I was busy preparing tea; Sri Aurobindo was still in bed. I noticed a carriage passing by my window and the whole house was in a bustle. I came out only to know that the Maharaja sahib had come and was quietly gone,

---

[33]Purani, A.B., *The Life of Sri Aurobindo*, Sri Aurobindo Ashram, 1978, p. 39.

hearing that Sri Aurobindo was still in bed and giving strict
instruction not to disturb him. He came back from his drive
in the park after an hour and Sri Aurobindo went out to meet
His Highness just as he was in his dhoti and bare body.[34]

It was during this visit to Kashmir that Aurobindo had another
spiritual experience. This occurred at the Shankaracharya Hill,
on top of which stands a temple built by Adi Shankarcharya. The
experience is vividly recalled in the poem 'Adwaita':

I walked on the high-wayed Seat of Solomon
Where Shankaracharya's tiny temple stands
Facing Infinity from Time's edge, alone
On the bare ridge, alone
On the bare ridge ending earth's vain romance.
Around me was a formless solitude:
All had become one strange Unnamable,
An unborn sole Reality world-nude,
Topless and fathomless, for ever still.
A Silence that was Being's only word,
The unknown beginning and the voiceless end
Abolishing all things moment-seen or heard,
On an incommunicable summit reigned,
A lonely Calm and void unchanging Peace
On the dumb crest of Nature's mysteries.[35]

The Maharaja gave Aurobindo a certificate in which he commended
his intelligence and tartly observed that he could probably be
more punctual and regular than he was. The certificate reads: 'His
Highness is pleased to note that he has found Mr Ghose a very

---

[34]Ghose, Barin, *Sri Aurobindo (as I understand him)*, unpublished manuscript, Sri
Aurobindo Archives.
[35]*The Complete Works of Sri Aurobindo: Volume 2: Collected Poems*, Sri Aurobindo
Ashram, 1997, p. 621.

useful and capable young man. With a little more of regularity and punctual habits he can be of much greater help; and it is hoped that Mr Ghose will be careful in future not to injure his own interests by any lack of these useful qualities.'[36] Why did the Maharaja tolerate such an insubordinate and irritating employee? There was clearly more than a measure of respect between the two. The Maharaja probably recognized that his unusual secretary was a cut above the kind of officials found either in the princely states or British provinces. It seems the quality of the work that Aurobindo did outweighed any possible inconveniences that he caused the Maharaja.

Family Connections

Shortly after arriving in India, Aurobindo had made contact with his family in Bengal. Brothers Benoybhushan and Manmohan, too, had returned to India by this time. Benoybhushan was employed by the Maharaja of Cooch-Behar as a tutor to his son, while Manmohan ended up as a professor of English at Dacca University. In 1894, Aurobindo took leave and first met Benoybhushan in Ajmer, where he was staying with his pupil, the prince. He finally reached Deoghar in Bengal, where Raj Narain Bose was living out his retirement. Aurobindo remembered the old man: 'I was at Deoghar and saw my grandfather there, first in good health and then bedridden with paralysis.' He discounted a view that he had been influenced by Raj Narain's philosophy:

> I don't think my grandfather was much of a philosopher; at any rate he never talked to me on the subject. My politics were shaped before I came to India; he talked to me of his Nationalist activities in the past, but I learned nothing new

[36]Cited in: Heehs, Peter, *The Lives of Sri Aurobindo*, Columbia University Press, 2008, p. 65.

from them. I had gone in England far beyond his stock of
ideas which belonged to an earlier period.[37]

Nevertheless, when Raj Narain died in 1899, Aurobindo wrote
a poem in his memory, 'In Transiit, Non Pareit', which revealed
his deep affection for his grandfather.

> *Not in annihilation lost, nor given*
> *To darkness are thou fled from us and light;*
> *O strong and sentient spirit; no mere heaven*
> *Of ancient joys, no silence cremate*
> *Received thee; but the omnipresent Thought*
> *Of which thou wast a part and earthly hour,*
> *Took back its gift, Into that splendor caught*
> *Thou hast not lost thy special brightness. Power*
> *Remains with thee and the old genial force*
> *Unseen for blinding light, not darkly lurks,*
> *As when a sacred river in its course,*
> *Dives into ocean, there its strength abides,*
> *Not less because with vastness wed and works*
> *Unnoticed in the grandeur of the tides.*[38]

Aurobindo did not know anyone among those milling around
him when he reached Raj Narain's house, and the old man finally
embraced his long-lost grandson and welcomed him home.
Aurobindo also met his mother for the first time since he had been
left behind in England. It must have been an intensely emotional
meeting, especially since Swarnalata at first refused to acknowledge
him. She insisted that her son was a small boy and relented only
when she saw a cut on his finger, the result of a childhood accident.

---

[37]*Complete Works of Sri Aurobindo: Volume 36: Autobiographical Notes and Other
Writings of Historical Interest*, Sri Aurobindo Ashram, 1997, p. 45.
[38]*The Complete Works of Sri Aurobindo: Volume 2: Collected Poems*, Sri Aurobindo
Ashram, 1997, p. 282.

Aurobindo was also reunited with his younger sister Sarojini and met his youngest brother, Barin, for the first time. Both of them have left their impressions of him at this time. Sarojini recalled, 'First came a telegram, then arrived Sejda [Bengali for third brother]. A very young and delicate face, shoulder-length hair cut in English fashion, Sejda was a very shy person. When womenfolk surrounded him, he shrank bashfully. Dadababu put his arm around him and embraced him in a warm welcome.'[39] Barin later wrote: 'Sejada as we called him, was a strange friend for me, at once a playmate and guide, with a quiet and absorbed look and almost always lost in thought.' Barin tried to get Aurobindo to come down from his rarefied heights: 'I remember how I used to tease him out of his books and day-dreams and he used to chase me about, pretending an anger he never felt.'[40]

Aurobindo appears to have developed a close relationship with his relatives on his mother's side. This can be gauged from the affectionate and bantering tone of a letter he wrote to Sarojini on his return to Baroda:

> It will be, I fear, quite impossible to come to you again so early as the Puja, though if I only could, I should start tomorrow. Neither my affairs, nor my finances will admit of it. Indeed, it was a great mistake for me to go at all; for it has made Baroda quite intolerable for me. There is an old story about Judas Iscariot, which suits me down to the ground. Judas, after betraying Christ, hanged himself and went to hell where he was honoured with the hottest oven in the whole establishment. However, since he had done one good deed in his life, Judas had the chance of sitting at the North Pole for an hour on every Christmas. 'Now

[39]Ghose, J.C., *Life-Work of Sri Aurobindo*, Atmashakti Library, 1929.
[40]Ghose, Barin, *Sri Aurobindo (as I understand him)*, unpublished manuscript, Sri Aurobindo Archives.

this has always seemed to me to me not mercy but, but a peculiar refinement of cruelty. For how could Hell fail to be ten times more Hell to the poor wretch after the delicious coolness of his iceberg? I do not know for what enormous crime I have been condemned to Baroda, but my case is just parallel. Since my pleasant sojourn with you... Baroda seems a thousand times Baroda. I infer from your letter that you are making great progress in English. I hope you will learn very quickly; I can then write to you quite what I want to say and just in the way I want to say it. I feel some difficulty in doing that now and I know and I don't know whether you will understand it.[41]

From Deoghar, Aurobindo went to Calcutta, where he stayed with his aunt and her husband, Krishna Kumar Mitra. This was to be a regular pattern during his visits, until he himself shifted base to Calcutta. Cousin Basanti remembered his first visit well:

Auro Dada used to arrive with two or three trunks. We always thought they would contain costly suits and other luxury items like scents. When he opened them I used to look and wonder. What is this? A few ordinary clothes and all the rest books and nothing but books! Does Auro Dada like to read all these? But because he liked this reading did not mean that he did not join us in our talks and our merrymaking. His talk used to be full of wit and humour.[42]

Aurobindo continued to meet members of his family on regular visits to Bengal. According to a letter that he wrote to Jogedra Bose, his uncle, in 1902, he also began to send a part of his salary for the maintenance of his mother and Sarojini, after

---

[41]*Complete Works of Sri Aurobindo: Volume 36: Autobiographical Notes and Other Writings of Historical Interest*, Sri Aurobindo Ashram, 1997, p. 123.
[42]Ghose, J.C., *Life-Work of Sri Aurobindo*, Atmashakti Library, 1929.

Manmohan stopped sending money. Aurobindo cryptically later said that Benoybhushan had to maintain his lifestyle at the court of Cooch-Behar, and that Manmohan had married, an expensive proposition, which were the reasons behind their financial backsliding.

Professor Ghose

When Aurobindo returned to Baroda from his leave, he found himself increasingly disinterested in the administrative process. He was more interested in teaching at Baroda College. He first taught French part-time in 1897, though an idea to move to the college full-time was stillborn. The situation took a turn in Aurobindo's favour when, in 1898, the English teacher, Littledale, went on long leave. Aurobindo found himself acting professor of English literature. He remained in the post till 1901. Later, in 1904, he became the vice principal, and then acting principal of Baroda College. He remained with the college until his departure from Baroda in 1906.

The college was run on British lines, with subjects tilted in favour of those that aligned with the interests of the British Raj. Despite the ferocious pressure of work at Cambridge University, Aurobindo had enjoyed the experience. In an address at Baroda College in 1899, he extolled the virtues of Oxford and Cambridge:

I think there is no student of Oxford or Cambridge who does not look back in after days on the few years of his undergraduate life as, of all the scenes he has moved in, that which calls up the happiest memories, and it is not surprising that this should be so, when we remember what that life must have meant to him. He goes up from the restricted life of his home and school and finds himself in surroundings which with astonishing rapidity expand his intellect, strengthen his character, develop his social faculties, force out all his abilities and turn him in three years from a boy into a man.[43]

There was a huge gap between the picture that he created and the reality of university education in India. Aurobindo was constrained to acknowledge that the quality of the students who came to Baroda College to prepare for the examinations of Bombay University for a degree was quite low—they were ignorant and did not have a real understanding of English. Aurobindo's experience of teaching left him close to despair. After giving an introductory lecture, he would proceed to discuss the assigned text. To his astonishment, he would find the students scribbling down every word of his. Soon, Aurobindo got into the habit of asking students to repeat the ending of the previous lecture, and he would continue from there. Rote learning, rather than original thought, was the norm. The students would sometimes tell him that what he was telling them was different from the notes that they had got from elsewhere—Aurobindo said that he was not bothered by the difference.

We can form a picture of Aurobindo as a teacher from the recollections of some of his students. Sanker Balwant Didmishe wrote: 'His mastery of the English language was phenomenal. Sometimes he examined our composition books. He wrote on them such remarks as "Fit for Standard III" and "How have you come to the College?"'[44] R.N. Patikar, another student, having read something by Thomas Babbington Macaulay, asked Aurobindo if he should imitate his style. Aurobindo told him that he would then only be an echo of Macaulay and should

---

[43]*Complete Works of Sri Aurobindo: Volume 1: Early Cultural Writings*, Sri Aurobindo Ashram, 1997, p. 353.

[44]Cited in: Roshan and Apurva (eds), *Sri Aurobindo in Baroda*, Sri Aurobindo Ashram Publications Division, 1993, p. 78.

instead cultivate his own thinking and style of writing.

Once, K.M. Munshi, who went on to become a senior Congress leader, asked him how nationalism was to be developed. Aurobindo pointed at a map of India and said words that were to echo across India in just a few years:

> Look at the map. Learn to find in it the portrait of Bharatmata. The cities, mountains, rivers and forests are the materials which go to make up her body. The people inhabiting the country are the cells which go to make up her living tissues. Our literature is her memory and speech. The spirit of her culture is her soul. The happiness and freedom of her children is her salvation. Behold Bharat as a living Mother, meditate upon her and worship her...[45]

The anthromorphization of India was to become a leitmotif of Aurobindo's writings and thinking in the next few years.

What was Aurobindo's life like outside the walls of bureaucracy and the halls of academe? We have much information from the pen of Dinendra Kumar Roy, who was brought in from Bengal to help Aurobindo improve his grasp of Bengali. A young teacher and writer, he was chosen for the job by Jogendra Bose. Roy's first encounter with Aurobindo left him unimpressed. He wrote:

> Before I met Aurobindo I had pictured him as a stout young man, bespectacled and dressed from head to toe in European clothes; rude in speech and, arrogant of eye and terribly haughty in temper.' The reality turned out to be very different: 'It goes without saying that I was disappointed with my first meeting with Aurobindo. Old-fashioned slippers with ends turned up on his feet; his clothes of coarse, flounced

---

[45]Roshan and Apurva (eds), *Sri Aurobindo in Baroda*, Sri Aurobindo Ashram Publications Division, 1993.

Ahmedabad-mill khadi, the end of his dhoti hanging loose, a tight-fitting waistcoat on his back; on his head, a mane of long, thin hair parted in the middle and hanging down over the neck; tiny pockmarks on his face; his eyes with a gentle, dreamy look—who would have thought that this thin, dark-skinned young man was Sriman Aurobindo Ghose... [46]

Aurobindo's lifestyle was very simple, almost spartan. For his official duties, the standard white suits and Gujarati caps and turbans were de rigueur. At home and with friends, as Roy noted, his dress was very casual. Aurobindo's diet was also very frugal. He took rice, bread, fish or meat. Sometimes, he took only vegetarian food. Later in life, he turned vegetarian. At meals, he usually also had a cigar and journal at hand. Patikar related an interesting anecdote about Aurobindo's eating habits. 'When he was absorbed in reading, he could be wholly oblivious of his surroundings. One evening his servant brought his meals with the words, "Master, the meal is served". "All right" was the answer. But an hour later, the servant found that the master was still reading, the dishes on the table being untouched!'[47] He would eat whatever was placed before him, however badly cooked others found it to be. Aurobindo's sleeping arrangements were equally spartan—a cast-iron bed with a thin mattress thrown on it. Only on the coldest of nights would he cover himself with a thin blanket.

Money was another matter of indifference. Aurobindo would place all the money that he received on a large tray and leave it there for anyone to take as needed. It was not kept under lock or key, and he kept no account of it. When asked by Patikar as to why he left the money around openly, Aurobindo said that it proved that they were living among good and honest people. He further

---

[46] Roy, Dinendra Kumar, *With Aurobindo in Baroda*, Sri Aurobindo Ashram, 2006.
[47] Roshan and Apurva (eds), *Sri Aurobindo in Baroda*, Sri Aurobindo Ashram Publications Division, 1993, p. 88.

said that he did not keep accounts because that job was for God! The Divine, apparently, gave him enough for his needs and kept the rest! These comments have shades of things soon to come.

Aurobindo's generosity was startling. Roy once saw him making out a money order form. Roy had been thinking of asking Aurobindo for some money to send home, and did so. Aurobindo pulled out some money, put away his own form, and told Roy to fill out a money order form and send the money. He overrode Roy's protests, and sat down to write a poem.

Aurobindo was, of course, a bibliomaniac—he read enormously during his years in Baroda. As we have seen, he carried books with him everywhere he went. They came from the top bookshops in Bombay and Calcutta, who had a deposit account in his name. Every month, as soon as his pay came, Aurobindo would send off orders for books chosen from a checklist sent to him. The books would come in large packing cases rather than parcels, such was their number. Aurobindo read three or four books simultaneously. He would finish all the books within eight to 10 days—then immediately order a fresh batch.

What were the books that he ordered and read? Roy saw books scattered all over his residence—on shelves, heaped in corners, piled on top of trunks or shoved into cupboards. The books were mostly related to English literature. Roy saw a collection of English poets—from Chaucer to Swinburne. We can imagine the range and breadth of Aurobindo's reading by looking at the 155 books from the Baroda years that he donated to the National College in Calcutta. They include books on poetry, novels, literary biographies, history, travel and philosophy. There were also works of Sanskrit and Bengali, including the Mahabharata and the writings of Bankim Chandra Chatterjee and Michael Madhusudan Dutt.

Aurobindo was in the habit of noting down titles of the books he bought, and also what he was reading at a particular time, how many pages he had read and even how much time it took him! For instance, in September 1900, he read 54 suktas containing 1,533 slokas of the Viratparva of the Mahabharata—in eight days. In the following three days, he read thrice the first part of Kalidasa's *Meghaduta*. At the same time, he was correcting examination papers and reading other books in Sanskrit, English and German as well as writing.

Aurobindo's passion lay in writing, and in Baroda, he laid the foundations for his future reputation as a writer. However, it is ironic that only a little amount of what he wrote at this time was actually published in Aurobindo's lifetime or under his name, much of it may also have been lost, except for *Pereseus the Deliverer*. A few small collections of poems also appeared but did not garner much attention until a collected edition was published in the 1940s. An evenly balanced lengthy appreciation of the Bengali writer Bankim Chandra Chatterjee was published, but at the end of the essay, in place of the writer's signature, appeared one word—'Zero'. A few essays on the ancient Sanskrit writer Kalidasa were probably the only ones which bore his name. Among his unpublished and incomplete writings are partial translations from the Ramayana and the Mahabharata— Aurobindo wrote extensively on them. The incomplete series of political essays that he wrote in *Indu Prakash* in 1893 acquired a semi-legendary status but were published anonymously. It was only in the 1950s that the fact of Aurobindo's authorship came to be known. Nevertheless, all of these formed the basis of what we can call Aurobindo's cultural nationalism.

Marriage and Family Life

The early years of the twentieth century saw two major events take place in Aurobindo's life, with far-reaching consequences. Having reached the ripe age of 28, as a result of a combination of familial pressure and his own desire, Aurobindo decided to get married. It was already a late age for marriage in India at that time. Aurobindo, being Bengali, decided that his wife, too, should be Bengali. The reason was probably that Bengali women, according to Aurobindo, 'are certainly the most tenderest, purest & most gracious & loving in the whole world'.[48] An advertisement was published in the papers, as was the norm, sometime in early 1900. Aurobindo received some 50 replies and went to Calcutta to choose his bride. After meeting many a prospect, he finally arrived at the house of Bhupal Chandra Bose and immediately chose his daughter, Mrinalini.

Mrinalini was 14, half of Aurobindo's age, and an age considered, at the time, to be a little old for a bride. She was beautiful, with rosy cheeks and curly hair. Bhupal Chandra Bose was a state agricultural officer, and later, the co-founder of Bangabasi College. In a 1931 memoir of his daughter, he wrote that Mrinalini was privately educated and at the Brahmo Girl's School until her marriage. Bose wrote, 'She evinced no exceptional abilities or tendencies at this age, indeed at no stage of her life'.[49] Mrinalini, though surrounded by Brahmos, evinced no interest in their doctrine. She, instead, seemed to be attracted by the teachings of Sri Ramakrishna and his disciple, Swami Vivekananda.

The marriage was solemnized on 29 April 1901 in Calcutta. It took place in accordance with Hindu rites and not that of the Brahmo Samaj, as Aurobindo believed that it was Hinduism that reflected the true nature of India. Amongst the guests were luminaries such as Lord Sinha and the scientist Jagadish Chandra Bose. A comedy of sorts took place when Aurobindo, as one having returned from abroad, was asked to undergo a rite of

---

[48]*Complete Works of Sri Aurobindo: Volume 1: Early Cultural Writings*, Sri Aurobindo Ashram, 1997, p. 153.
[49]Heehs, Peter, *The Lives of Sri Aurobindo*, Columbia University Press, 2008.

purification before the marriage ceremony. Aurobindo politely refused to do so. Finally, a priest was found who, for a suitable sum, took the purification as having been done. The newly-weds then went to Deoghar, followed by Nainital (to attend on the Gaekwad) and then proceeded to Baroda, with Sarojini in tow as a companion to Mrs Ghose.

It is difficult, if not impossible, to reconstruct the story of Aurobindo's marriage in full. Mrinalini's short life is shadowy. There were no children, and even before Aurobindo's abrupt departure from Baroda, she spent a lot of time with her family in the east. It was not just the age difference—Aurobindo's Bengali was patchy, and Mrinalini's English poor. Communication was difficult at times. The difference in education was also stark. Aurobindo's activities in Baroda and later in Calcutta were not conducive to the kind of stable family life that Mrinalini would have expected, as Aurobindo admitted in a 1906 letter to his father-in-law:

> I am afraid I shall never be good for much in the way of domestic virtues. I have tried, very ineffectively, to do some part of my duty as a son, a brother, and a husband, but there is something in me which subordinates everything else to it. Of course, that is no excuse for my culpability in not writing letters—a fault I am afraid I will always be quicker to admit than reform. I can easily understand that to others it may seem to spring from the lack of the most ordinary affections... I fear you must take me as I am with all my imperfections on my head.[50]

But write to her he did, though only a handful of those letters seem to have survived, one of them written in English. One letter that Aurobindo wrote to Mrinalini was confiscated at the time of his

---

[50]*Complete Works of Sri Aurobindo: Volume 36: Autobiographical Notes and Other Writings of Historical Interest*, Sri Aurobindo Ashram, 1997, p. 147.

arrest in Calcutta. A translation of the letter was produced in court and created a sensation, though it was in no way germane to the trial. The letter, however, gives us an unparalleled and revealtory insight into Aurobindo's psyche at this time. Aurobindo wrote the letter on 30 August 1905 in reply to a letter from Mrinalini about a death in her family. He wrote:

> I think you have understood by now that the man with whose fate yours has been linked is a man of a very unusual character. Mine is not the same field of action, the same purpose in life, the same mental attitude as that of the people of today in this country. I am in every respect different from them and out of the ordinary. Perhaps you know what ordinary men say of an extraordinary view, an extraordinary endeavour, an extraordinary ambition. To them it is madness; only, if the madman is successful in his work then he is called no more a madman but a great genius.[51]

He added the prophetic words, 'Not to speak of success I have not yet even entirely entered my field of work.' He said that Mrinali should consider him a madman, and thus herself unfortunate, for a 'woman's expectations are all bound up in worldly happiness and sorrow. A madman will not make his wife happy, he can only make her miserable.' He then asked her if she would follow him, as expected of a wife in the Hindu tradition.

Aurobindo then came to the heart of his letter, which created consternation in court as it was read out loud—he spoke of his 'three madnesses'.

> The first one is this. I firmly believe that the accomplishments, genius, higher education and learning and wealth that God has given me are His. I have a right to spend for my own purposes only what is needed for the maintenance of the

---

[51]Sri Aurobindo, *Bengali Writings*, Sri Aurobindo Ashram, 1997.

family and is otherwise absolutely essential. The rest must be returned to God. If I spend everything for myself, for my pleasure and luxury, I am a thief.

And the second 'madness', which he said had only recently seized him, was:

It is this: by whatever means, I must have the direct vision of God. Religion these days means repeating the name of God at any odd hour, praying in public, showing off how pious one is. I want nothing of this. If God exists, there must be someway to experience His existence, to meet Him face to face. However ardous this path is, I have made up my mind to follow it.

And then the final climatic 'madness':

My third madness is that while others look upon their country as an inert piece of matter—a few meadows and fields, forests and hills and rivers—I look upon Her as the Mother. What would a son do if a demon sat on his mother's breast and started sucking her blood? Would he quietly sit down to his dinner, amuse himself with his wife and children, or would he rush out to deliver his mother? I know I have the strength to deliver this fallen race. It is not physical strength—I am not going to fight with sword or gun—but it is the strength of knowledge.

Aurobindo then made the extraordinary claim that this idea to free India had first come to him when he was 14, and that it had matured in him by the time he had reached the age of 18.

Aurobindo then went on to say, clearly referring to secret revolutionary activities, that:

After listening to what my aunt said you formed the idea that some wicked people had dragged your simple and innocent husband onto the bad path. But it was this innocent husband of yours who brought those people and hundreds of others on to that path, be it bad or good, and will yet bring thousands of others on to that same path. I do not say that the work will be accomplished in my lifetime, but it certainly will be done.

He concluded the letter by exhorting Mrinalini to be his shakti (female power) and to develop her faith in him through prayer. The letter makes clear that, as we have already seen, Aurobindo did not set much store by money. It confirms that both his spiritual and underground political activity were in full flow and that they were known to both his wife and other members of his family. The tone of confidence, and the clarity and precision of his self-analysis cannot but fascinate. All the three traits that he spoke of lasted all his life and made Aurobindo a force to reckon with in the political and spiritual life landscape of India.

The rest of Mrinalini's sad and short life is easily told, even though it falls in a later part of Aurobindo's life. She accompanied him to Calcutta and moved from house to house with him, but spent more and more time with her family. She never lived with him again after his arrest, though she saw him in jail, accompanied by her father. When Aurobindo left Calcutta forever, in 1910, she was not aware of it, and learnt his whereabouts much later. During this time, she became very devout and used to meet Sarada Devi, the revered wife of Sri Ramakrishna, from whom she is said to have received diksha. Sarda Devi told her that Aurobindo was a mahayogi (great yogi). While arrangements were being made for her departure to Pondicherry, she perished in the flu epidemic of 1918. Aurobindo wrote a poignant letter to his father-in-law:

I have not written to you with regard to this fatal event in both our lives; words are useless in face of the feelings it has caused, if even they can ever express our deepest emotions. God has seen good to lay upon me the one sorrow that could still touch me to the centre. He knows better than ourselves what is best for each of us, and now the first sense of the irreparable has passed, I can bow with submission to His divine purpose. The physical tie between us is, as you say, severed; but the tie of affection subsists for me. Where I have once loved, I do not cease from loving. Besides, she who was the cause of it, still is near though not visible to our physical vision.[52]

The question again arises: why did Aurobindo marry, if he had set himself on a hard path? He gave the answer himself to Nirodbaran, his secretary and personal physician, in a brief letter in 1936: 'Do you think Buddha or Confucius or myself were born with a prevision that they or I would take to the spiritual life? So long as one is in the ordinary consciousness, one lives the ordinary life—when the awakening and the new consciousness come, one leaves—nothing puzzling in that.'[53]

Experiments in Spirituality and Revolution

One day, a few months after Aurobindo's marriage, the servant brought into Aurobindo's presence a dirty, dishevelled, bedraggled young man, covered with coal and dust. Aurobindo took one look at him and sent him off to bathe. It was Barin. After studying at colleges in Patna and Dacca, he had tried his hand at farming, in which he failed. He then opened a teashop in Patna, which, too, went under. Having, by then, worn out his welcome with the two eldest brothers, he made his way to Baroda. At Baroda, he engaged in drawing, painting, playing music, hunting and gardening.

---

[52]*Complete Works of Sri Aurobindo: Volume 36: Autobiographical Notes and Other Writings of Historical Interest*, Sri Aurobindo Ashram, 1997, p. 147.
[53]Nirodbaran, *Correspondence with Sri Aurobindo*, vol. 1, Sri Aurobindo Ashram Press, 1969, p. 576.

Barin also dabbled in the paranormal. He had come across a book on spiritism—the practice of calling up the spirits of the dead. This was done using a planchette and séances, practices quite popular in England and Europe. Barin, apparently, had some success with the automatic writing, conjuring up some matter written in excellent English, according to Sri Aurobindo. Aurobindo later tried automatic writing in Calcutta, calling up the spirit of Raja Rammohun Roy. The writing was later published as *Yoga Sadhan*. Aurobindo always disclaimed it as his writing, or as an expression of his thinking at the time. As for the séances, according to Sri Aurobindo, they once heard from their father, his identity being confirmed by a gold watch given to Barin. Aurobindo did not take much interest in these events, but they are important in that they informed the young agnostic of the existence of realms and forces beyond the material world.

While leading a startlingly busy life, with almost every minute of his day filled with college work, the Maharaja's work, home life, meeting friends and writing, Aurobindo also began to investigate spirituality and yoga, spurred on by his discovery of Indian philosophy and religion in England and now India, and also to understand the experiences that he had had over the years. If that programme was not enough, he had also embarked on the project that he had set his mind on long ago in England—the liberation of India from alien rule. The spiritual aspiration and the commencement of covert political activities were near-simultaneous in time and were inextricably cross-connected. The one reinforced the other until Aurobindo's sudden exit from the political stage.

The impetus for both came from within the small group of people Aurobindo had befriended, among them, his old Cambridge comrade, Deshpande. After a stint in Bombay as the editor of *Indu Prakash*, he had joined the Baroda Service. Deshpande, having had some experience of yoga, had offered to help Aurobindo.

While reading the Mahabharata, Ramayana and the Upanishads, Aurobindo had been dissatisfied with the commentaries on them and felt that something more was needed to understand them. That something, he thought, might be yoga. However, he declined Deshpande's offer, as he felt that it would mean a withdrawal from the world, something he was not prepared to do at the point of time.

The spontaneous spiritual experiences that had occurred earlier continued. Aurobindo owned a strange-looking horse-drawn carriage, which often attracted attention from passers-by. Once, while riding in it, he had a premonition of an accident, but it never took place. At about this time, it seems that Aurobindo consulted another friend of his, A.B. Devdhar, who was a disciple of Swami Brahmananda of Chandod. Aurobindo had now realized that if the power of yoga could be used while turning away from life, it could also be directed towards his primary aim—the liberation of India. As Sri Aurobindo acknowledged later, 'I learnt that Yoga gives power, and I thought why the devil I should not get the power and use it to liberate my country? It was something from behind which got the idea accepted by the mind: mine was a side-door entry into the Spiritual Life.'[54]

After a séance in which the spirit of Sri Ramakrishna said '*mandir gado* (build a temple)', Aurobindo and the others took it as a literal order (Aurobindo later mused that it might have been metaphorical—to build a temple within oneself). Aurobindo, Deshpande and Devdhar went to Chandod, where they met Swami Brahmananda. Aurobindo was greatly impressed by the Swami, who was said to have been 100 years old. While Aurobindo visited him a number of times over the years, Brahmananda was never his guru. Brahmananda always kept his eyes closed during meetings, but on the last occasion that Aurobindo saw him, he suddenly opened his eyes and looked directly at Aurobindo. Aurobindo

---

[54]Purani, A.B., *Evening Talks with Sri Aurobindo*, Sri Aurobindo Ashram, 2007.

was struck by the the beauty of his eyes, and it remained an unforgettable experience for him.

At Chandod, Deshpande opened a school at Ganganath, run on nationalist lines, where Sanskrit was also taught. According to a 1909 Criminal Intelligence Circular, the school was supported by an anarchist group of Calcutta and there are '37 students on the rolls of the school which consists of two divisions, Vedic and Vehabaric. To the former, instruction is given in the Vedas and modern science. The latter are taught their mother-tongue, Hindi, Sanskrit, English, modern history and Science.'[55]

It was probably at this time that Aurobindo wrote a revolutionary pamphlet, *Bhawani Mandir*. It was published clandestinely and distributed through Aurobindo's supporters. It spoke of creating an organization of sadhus who would dedicate themselves to the liberation of the country, personified as the Goddess Bhawani. The pamphlet made out the need for such an organization and the manner in which it was to be run. The idea for such an organization came from Barin, who hunted for a site where it could be set up. He was probably inspired by reading Bankim's novel *Anandamath* in which such an organization existed. The British were aware of the pamphlet and the interest it engendered amongst those who had got hold of a copy. There were reports of translations into Hindi and Tamil, which would have spread the message far and wide. The British, thus, banned it.

Devdhar taught Aurobindo the basics of pranayama in 1904, and he practised assiduously. Sri Aurobindo later recalled:

Prananyama does not bring dullness in the brain. My own experience, on the contrary, is that the brain becomes illumined. When I was practicing Pranayama at Baroda, I used to do it for about five hours in the day—three hours

---

[55]Roshan and Apurva (eds), *Sri Aurobindo in Baroda*, Sri Aurobindo Ashram Publications Division, 1993, p. 132.

in the morning and two in the evening. I found that that the mind began to work with great illumination and power. I used to write poetry in those days. Before the Pranayama practice, usually I wrote five to eight lines per day, about 200 lines in a month. After the practice I could write 200 lines within half an hour.[56]

He found that he could also remember all the lines and write them down at any time. Clearly, for Aurobindo, creativity and memory had been enhanced.

Aurobindo's spirtitual quest, originally, was not an end in itself—it was a means to political liberation. In a note on his political life written in the third person and first published in 1948, Sri Aurobindo spoke of the three distinct strands that ran through his political life:

There were three sides to Sri Aurobindo's political ideas and activities. First, there was the action with which he started, a secret revolutionary propaganda and organization of which the central object was the preparation of an armed insurrection. Secondly, there was a public propaganda intended to convert the whole nation to the ideal of independence which was regarded, when he entered into politics, by the vast majority of Indians as unpractical and impossible, an almost insane chimera. It was thought that the British Empire was too powerful and India too weak, effectively disarmed and impotent even to dream of the success of such an endeavour. Thirdly, there was the organization of the people to carry on a public and united opposition and undermining of the foreign rule through an increasing non-cooperation and passive resistance.[57]

---

[56]Purani, A.B., *Evening Talks with Sri Aurobindo*, Sri Aurobindo Ashram, 2007.
[57]*Complete Works of Sri Aurobindo: Volume 36: Autobiographical Notes and Other*

The first and second lines of Aurobindo's political activities began almost simultaneously. Shortly after Aurobindo returned to India, Deshpande, then in Bombay, as the editor of the journal *Indu Prakash*, asked him to write an article on the Indian National Congress. Aurobindo duly complied and sent in an article with the innocent title 'India and the British Parliament'. Published anonymously on 26 June 1893, it spoke of a recent vote lost by the Liberal government on a matter of policy related to India—the holding of civil service examinations simultaneously in England and India. Aurobindo derided the rejoicing with which it was received by the Indian press:

> A great critic has pronounced that the aim of all truly helpful criticism is to see the object as it really is… in India, whose destinies are in the balance, and at a time when a straw might turn the scale, it is of the gravest importance that no delusion, however specious or agreeable, should be allowed. Yet in the face of this necessity, the Indian Press seems eager to accept even the flimsiest excuse for deluding itself. The simple truth of the matter is that we shall not get from the British Parliament anything than nominal redress, or at the most a petty and tinkering legislation.[58]

All of the elements of Aurobindo's mature style are here—clarity of thought and argument, evisceration without vituperation, sarcasm and humour. The article caused a stir among those who had access to it. But it still was a mere trailer for the storm that was to come. The editor, delighted by the consternation among readers, asked Aurobindo to write a series of articles addressing some of the issues he had raised about how to get redress from the British.

Writings of Historical Interest, Sri Aurobindo Ashram, 1997, p. 47.
[58]*Complete Works of Sri Aurobindo: Volume 6: Bande Mataram — I–II*, Sri Aurobindo Ashram, 1997, p. 7.

Nine articles were published as a series titled 'New Lamps for Old' from 7 August 1893 to 6 March 1894. The articles inaugurated a new phase in Indian political journalism. Nothing like them had been seen before. Aurobindo trained his guns on the loyalist leadership of the Indian National Congress and coined the legendary and inflammatory phrase of derision that described the Congress policy as 'petition and prayer'. Disturbed and outraged by the tone and tenor of these articles by the unknown new kid on the block, official circles began to take an interest in his identity. Mahadev Govid Ranade—social reformer, Congress leader and jurist—advised the proprietor of *Indu Prakash* of the official interest. He, in turn, put pressure on Deshpande to moderate the tone of the articles. Aurobindo reluctantly did so, and soon after, lost interest. He stopped writing the articles, leaving the series incomplete. Ranade asked to meet the young author. He advised Aurobindo that he should put his undoubted talents to other use—such as prison reform! Aurobindo's authorship was known to only a few in Bombay and Baroda, but the series had sent a shockwave through the Congress, which quickly subsided. The articles were disinterred and published under Sri Aurobindo's name for the first time in the 1950s. They are seen by historians as a precursor of the militant challenge that was building up in the Congress. The question of how influential they actually were at the time is impossible to answer.

The unknown public intellectual making waves was also secretly working on creating an underground revolutionary organization. Would such an organization, or smaller groups, have succeeded? Sri Aurobindo's thoughtful, considered evaluation almost 50 years after the event is worth understanding:

> At that time the military organization of the great empires and their means of military action were not so overwhelming and apparently irresistible as they now are: the rifle was

still the decisive weapon, air power had not developed and the force of artillery was not so devastating as it afterwards became. India was disarmed, but Sri Aurobindo thought that with proper organization and help from outside this difficulty might be overcome and in so vast a country as India and with the smallness of the regular British armies, even a guerilla warfare accompanied by general resistance and revolt might be effective. There was also the possibility of a great revolt in the Indian army.[59]

Aurobindo felt, based on his knowledge and understanding of the British, that being a pragmatic lot, they would quickly capitulate considering how heavily the odds weighed against them. Though they would resist a revolt and hand out piecemeal reforms, 'they were not the kind which would be ruthlessly adamantine to the end: if they found resistance and revolt becoming general and persistent they would in the end try to arrive at an accommodation to save what they could of their empire or in an extremity prefer to grant independence rather than have it forcefully wrested from their hands.'[60]

From the very beginning, Aurobindo decided that all means—constitutional, agitational, violent or non-violent—were to be used to achieve the ultimate goal of freedom. The question of violence and its use or otherwise was later the principal difference between Aurobindo and Mahatma Gandhi. In a 1948 note, Sri Aurobindo spoke sharply on the expediency of violence, a question which had recurred over and over, and had been addressed by him. Sri Aurobindo said:

In some quarters there is the idea that Sri Aurobindo's political standpoint was entirely pacifist, that he was

---

[59]*Complete Works of Sri Aurobindo: Volume 36: Autobiographical Notes and Other Writings of Historical Interest*, Sri Aurobindo Ashram, 1997, p. 47.
[60]Ibid. 47.

opposed in principle and in practice to all violence and that he denounced terrorism, insurrection etc. as entirely forbidden by the spirit and letter of Hindu religion. It is even suggested that he was a forerunner of the gospel of Ahimsa. This is quite incorrect. Sri Aurobindo is neither an impotent moralist nor a weak pacifist. ...Sri Aurobindo has never concealed his opinion that a nation is entitled to attain its freedom by violence, if it can do so or not, depends on what is the best policy, not on ethical considerations.[61]

The narrative of Aurobindo's work as a revolutionary organizer is shadowy, at times sketchy to the point of being almost invisible. The documentation is quite thin, but then if revolutionaries had maintained archives of the kind that gladden a historian's heart, their seizure by the police would have speeded the revolutionaries up the gallows steps. However, the scanty information that we have clearly points to the pioneering role Sri Aurobinbo played as an inspiration for the revolutionary movement in the country, especially Bengal. The myth of the revolutionary Aurobindo was to continue to inspire revolutionaries long after he had vanished from the field.

Aurobindo carried out his covert revolutionary organizational activities with utmost secrecy, all the while carrying out his official duties without a care. The first stirrings towards revolutionary activity took place within the confines of Aurobindo's small, intimate circle of friends. They included Deshpande, Madhavrao Jadhav (an officer in the Baroda State army), and his brother, Keshavrao. Barin was also let into this group, and he soon became an important instrument for the execution of Aurobindo's plans. The final element was the appearance of Jatindra Banerjee from Bengal. He had tried to join the army but was refused, being a Bengali. Jatin, with Madhavrao's help, was admitted into the

---

[61]Ibid.

Baroda army in 1898 after being declared as belonging to the United Provinces. Aurobindo had persuaded him to use his military training to instruct future recruits to the cause.

Aurobindo sent Barin and Jatin to recruit and train members under the cover of samitis or societies for lathi play, which had come up in Bengal. Aurobindo thought it would take 30 years for the results to fructify.

> The idea was to establish secretly or as far as possible as visible action could be taken, under various pretexts and covers, revolutionary propaganda and recruiting throughout Bengal. This was to be done among the youth of the country while sympathy, and support and financial and other assistance were to be obtained from the older men who had advanced views or could be won over to them... Young men were to be trained in activities which might be helpful for ultimate military action, such as riding, physical training, athletics of various kinds, drill and organised movement... As soon as the idea was sown, it attained a rapid prosperity... the few rapidly became many.[62]

But there were teething problems too. Barin and Jatin were unable to work together due to their differing temperaments. Barin also had an inability to take orders from anybody but his elder brother. At one point, Aurobindo had to sort out the issues between them. Nevertheless, the discord hampered the progress of the movement. Sri Aurobindo observed that his 'attempt at a closer organization of the whole movement did not succeed, but the movement itself did not suffer by that, for the general idea was taken up and activity of many separate groups led to a greater and more widespread diffusion of the revolutionary drive and its actions.'[63] It was these

---

[62]Ibid. 49.
[63]Ibid.

groups that were to be the backbone of the nationalist movement in Bengal in just a few years, and Sri Aurobindo, the public face of the protests against British rule.

There was a crucial element in the indoctrination provided to new recruits that Aurobindo insisted upon. One of the members of the revolutionary groups was Sakharam Ganesh Deuskar, who had written a Bengali book, *Desher Katha*. It recounted the economic exploitation of India by the British and had a considerable impact on people. Aurobindo seized upon this and propagated the concept of Swadeshi—literally, 'of our country'. Swadeshi meant the purchase and use of items only of products made in India by Indian manufacturers, thus ending the dependence on British goods. Sri Aurobindo noted that he himself 'had always considered the shaking off of this economic yoke and the development of Indian trade and industry as a necessary concomitant of the revolutionary endeavour.'[64] Swadeshi was to prove a potent weapon, and one which acquired importance at the national level. Mahatma Gandhi, with whose name Swadeshi is usually associated, had not yet entered the scene.

Aurobindo had undertaken a tour of Bengal with Devabrata Bose, an associate of Barin. After taking stock of the situation of the revolutionary groups and having sounded out prominent citizens on the feelings of the people, he came to a crucial conclusion. Sri Aurobindo said that 'his experience in this journey persuaded him that secret action or preparation by itself was not likely to be effective if there were not also a wide public movement which would create a universal patriotic fervor and popularize the idea of independence as the ideal and aim of Indian politics. It was this conviction that determined his later action.'[65]

---

[64]Ibid. 47.
[65]Ibid. 46.

It was this conviction that made him reach out to a rising star of the Indian National Congress—Bal Gangadhar Tilak, who belonged to Poona in the province of Bombay. After completing his education at Bombay University, he embarked on a career as an educationist and a fiery journalist. His Marathi paper, *Kesari*, sold in large numbers, eclipsing those published in English. Tilak became an influential opinion-maker and a constant thorn for British officials. Their wrath fell on him when he was imprisoned for 18 months for having written an article that supposedly inspired the killing of some officials. When Tilak went to jail, he was a well-known journalist. He came out to be greeted as a national hero. Tilak was a member of the Indian National Congress but led a group that opposed the official policies of the Congress and wanted a more militant political programme. Aurobindo had heard of him through Deshpande, who had been a member of Tilak's defence team at his trial.

Aurobindo sought out Tilak at the Ahmedabad session of the Congress in 1902. As Sri Aurobindo recalled, he 'contacted Tilak whom he regarded as the one possible leader for a revolutionary party and met him at the Ahmedabad Congress; there Tilak took him out of the pandal and talked to him for an hour in the grounds expressing his contempt for the Reformist movement and explaining his own line of action in Maharashtra.'[66] Aurobindo concluded that Tilak would do. Tilak also introduced Aurobindo to a secret society in Bombay set up by a Rajput nobleman. Aurobindo took the society's oath. He, thus, became a link between the revolutionary groups in Bengal and the educated militant nationalists of western India.

Among Aurobindo's papers, there is an incomplete essay, begun after attending the Congress session. In it, he wrote the obituary of the Congress of his day:

---

[66]Ibid. 47.

The political activity of the nation gathering itself into the form of the Congress rose for some time with noise and a triumphant surging impetus until like a wave as it culminates breaking upon rocks, it dashed itself against the hard facts of human nature & the elementary conditions of successful political action which the Congress leaders had never grasped or had chosen to ignore; there it stopped and now there is throughout the country the languor, the weakness, the tendency to break up & discohere of the retiring wave.[67]

Another fateful meeting took place when an Irish woman, Margaret Noble, came to Baroda to meet the Maharaja. She was better known as Sister Nivedita, the disciple of Swami Vivekananda. She had revolutionary links and had come in the hope of getting assistance from the Maharaja. She left disappointed. Aurobindo had gone to receive her at the railway station. Sister Nivedita had heard of Aurobindo, and he was aware of her.

While Aurobindo was ruminating on how to get the masses to wake up, imperial hubris delivered itself into his hands. West Bengal was dominated by Hindus, while in the eastern part of the state, Muslims predominated. The Viceroy, Lord Curzon, announced the partition of the state on 20 July 1905, giving the necessity of administrative efficiency as the reason for this unprecedented act. Bengal exploded. Aurobindo visited the state and came back in a state of high excitement. He wanted to be a part of the political action taking place in Bengal. Finally, in 1906, after 13 years in Baroda, he packed his bags, bid farewell to the Maharaja, and took the train to Calcutta and into history.

[67]*Complete Works of Sri Aurobindo: Volume 6: Bande Mataram—I-II*, Sri Aurobindo Ashram, 1997, p. 65.

3

The Culture of Nationalism

The years that Aurobindo had spent in Baroda were busy ones. It was during this time that he quietly slipped out of his European persona and seamlessly became an Indian. There was no abrupt trashing of European culture; instead, Aurobindo focused on rediscovering the elements of the culture into which he had been born and taken away from. The Indianization of Aurobindo is a remarkable event—it was a quiet transformation in which he retained the language and some of the ways of thinking of the West and merged it with the discoveries he made through his probing into the ancient Indian culture.

The result was a unique blend of culture and nationalism. It was not so much cultural nationalism, which is derided in academe today, but a culture of nationalism and a nationalism of culture. In short, it is an appreciation that the alien culture being foisted on India was not suited to the ethos of the country, and that its growth would be stunted. The nature of the culture necessary would arise from the psyche of India itself, and thus would be a culture rooted in the Indian mind and soil. Such a culture could not possibly prosper under alien rule. Thus, it was necessary for foreign rule to first be removed. For Aurobindo, culture and nationalism were not separate categories in the context of India. One needs the other in order to survive and achieve its potential. To achieve this objective, Aurobindo sought in the past the seeds of the future.

A Question of Culture

This question arose in Aurobindo's mind when he was studying the Upanishads and other Sanskrit texts. He found that while he had no problem studying their translations by western scholars, the same was not true when it came to the matter of interpretation. He found both Max Mueller and Paul Deussen unconvincing. The reason for this lay in their application of western principles and procedures of analysis to eastern works. Thus, a methodology that was developed to study the Greek and Roman literature and philosophy was being used to study the Ramayana and Mahabharata, totally ignoring the different cultural context in which they were written. This, of course, held the implication that western culture was superior, and thus could be applied as a tool and a standard anywhere in the world. Aurobindo's dissatisfaction was clear—a century before Edward Said, Aurobindo was saying something that was analogous to the Saidian concept of Orientalsim.

It is probably this situation that Aurobindo had in mind when he wrote in his essay on Kalidasa:

> It was the supreme misfortune of India that before she was
> able to complete the round of her experience and gather up
> the fruit of her long millenniums of travail by commencing a
> fourth and more perfect age in which moral, intellectual and
> material development should be all equally harmonized and
> all spiritualized, the inrush of barbarians broke in finally on
> her endless tapasya of effort and beat her national life into
> fragments...Will she yet arise, new combine her past and
> continue the great dream where she left it off, shaking off on

the one hand the soils and the filth that have grown on her in her period of downfall and futile struggle, and reasserting on the other her peculiar individuality and national type? In doing so lies her one chance of national salvation.[68]

The road to a revival of culture, and thus the life of the nation lay in the political field and through revolution. For only then would there be a positive environment conducive to the flowering of a new Indian culture. Aurobindo, as we have seen, wrote a number of politically charged articles and pamphlets. We have some idea of his economic views from the reports and speeches that he wrote for Maharaja Sayajirao Gaekwad. There are also some fragments, left incomplete and unpublished, which give some insight into the evolution of his political and nationalist ideas. Aurobindo's ideas on the economy are usually little referenced, but we can glean them from a report that he wrote on trade in Baroda and a speech he drafted on the revival of industry for the Maharaja.

Trade Report

The report was based upon data provided by the government of Baroda. The salient points of the report are presented in a section entitled 'General Suggestions' and clearly reflect Aurobindo's thinking. It must be remembered that the report was made at a time when famine and hunger were stalking Baroda. The report starts with a bang: 'Trade throughout the Raj is in a state of depression and decline. The great industries that once flourished, such as weaving, dyeing, Sharafi &c. are entirely broken and though a number of small retail trades have sprung up, the balance is greatly on the side of decline.'[69] He then listed the

---

[68]*Complete Works of Sri Aurobindo: Volume 1: Early Cultural Writings*, Sri Aurobindo Ashram, 1997, p. 166.
[69]Ibid. 725.

causes for this decline—European competition and that of towns such as Ahmedabad and Poona, introduction of machinery, and abandonment of traditional professions. He then listed the delicate causes of the 'continual drain of money' due to large purchases from Europe and Bombay, employment of officials from outside the Raj (in other words, non-Indians), and the preference for foreign rather than local contractors. The suggestions that he made for remedial measures add up to one word—Swadeshi. All efforts needed to be made in a single direction—the revival and improvement of local artisans, and to encourage them to raise the standard of their goods and services so that they prove to be more effective and offer competition to outsiders. He also called for simplification of taxes and tax concessions, and for students to be sent abroad to learn new techniques, the knowledge of which they would bring back and spread widely.

Industrial Revival

A speech given by the Maharaja on 15 December 1902 in Ahemdabad at the Industrial Exhibition was written by Aurobindo, and it is perhaps the clearest exposition of his economic thinking that we have. It was an audacious effort and probably made more than one official of the Raj pale at what the Maharaja was saying. In the very beginning, it was made clear that a turning point had been reached for the Indian economy:

> Famine, increasing poverty, widespread disease, all these bring home to us the fact that there is some radical weakness in our system and that something must be done to remedy it. But there is another and a larger aspect of the matter and that is that this economic problem is our last ordeal as a people. It is our last chance. Fail there and what can the future bring us? We can only grow poorer and weaker, more dependent on

foreign help; we must watch our industrial freedom fall into extinction and drag out a miserable existence as the hewers of wood and drawers of water to any foreign power which happens to be our master. Solve that problem and you have a great future before you, the future of a great people, worthy of your ancestors and of your old position among the nations.[70]

Having set the stage, the problem is then identified:

A country without flourishing manufacturers must always be a poor country. The future, therefore, imperatively claims this from us, that we shall cease to be a purely agricultural country and vindicate for ourselves some place at least among commercial and manufacturing nations. Otherwise we shall only establish for ourselves the unhappiness of unsatisfied cravings and the benumbing effects of an ideal to which we can make no approach.

Then came the first twist of the knife:

There is a theory which affects to regard the races inhabiting the tropical and subtropical regions of the earth as disinherited by some mysterious law of Nature from all hope of originality, enterprise and leadership. These things belong to the temperate regions; the tropics are to be for ever no more than the field for the energies of the superior races, to whom alone belong empire, civilisation, trade and manufacture. We are to be restricted to a humble subordination, a servile imitation, and to the production of raw materials for their markets.[71]

It was then conceded that this was the prevailing situation— all key sectors of the economy and governance were in the

---

[70]Ibid. 694.
[71]Ibid. 696.

hands of Europeans. Then a case was made that it had not always been like this, and that India had, not that long ago, been a much-envied land of wealth and originality. A caveat indicated that this originality, in recent years, was confined largely to the spiritual realm, citing the examples of Swami Dayanand Saraswati and Raja Rammohun Roy. Then it was pointed out that this was not exactly correct, for there had also been great warriors such as Shivaji, Hyderali and Ranjit Singh, who had shown their military genius in empire building. And when there were communities such as the Parsis, Bhatias, the Khojas and the merchants of Sind, astute traders all, why was there such a lack of Indians in trade and industry? It could be said that the western advances in science had propelled them forward—but prosperous Indian trade and industry had already disappeared before that occurred. So, what was the cause for the backwardness of the Indian economy?

The final thrust of the knife was thus: 'If we go a little deeper into the matter we find that there is a further reason which does not depend on the natural working of economic laws but which is political in its nature, the result of the acquisition of political power by the East India Company and the absorption of India into the growing British Empire.'[72]

The fault for such an event having come to pass lay with the Indians themselves: 'Our weakness lies in this that we have for many years lain prostrate under a fictitious sense of our own helplessness and made no adequate attempt to react against our circumstances. We have succumbed where we should have exhausted every possibility of resistance and remedy.'[73] Blame is laid squarely at the feet of the superstitions plaguing Indian society and religion, and no positive change can occur unless

---

[72]Ibid.
[73]Ibid.

they are shaken off. The solution, then, is also in the hands of the Indians:

> Then India may again be what she was in the past and what she is so admirably fitted by nature to be, a self-sufficing country; famous for artistic and useful industries. To raise her again to this should be the ideal of every patriotic citizen. But in order that the ideal be may be realised we need, first: knowledge of our possibilities, of the means and facilities necessary to success, and of the lines on which activity would be best repaid; and secondly: belief in ourselves and in each other so that our knowledge may not fail for want of cooperation.[74]

The rest of the two-hour speech then basically expanded upon the 'Trade Report', but in much greater length. It ended with the ironic pious hope for the continued good health of the British monarch!

The revival of cultural life and economic activity was obviously linked to political activity. Political activity, in the context of the British Empire in India, was, for all practical purposes, non-existent. There was only one national-level organization that could be reasonably described as a political party—the Indian National Congress, which was designed as a means for the newly emergent Indian middle class to express its views on national issues without upsetting the imperial applecart. The most prominent lawyers, educationists and businessmen from all parts of the country assembled at an annual meeting for a few days, in different cities every year. The Congress elected a president to preside over its sessions and passed resolutions on different subjects without discussion or debate. The resolutions were prepared by a small committee. The speeches were robustly loyal to the British without a quiver in phrase. The Raj and its officials

---

[74]Ibid. 702.

accepted its protestations of loyalty, ignored its requests and barely tolerated its existence. And as for the general population, few were aware of its existence.

Aurobindo's anonymous articles in *Indu Prakash* made clear his contempt for the political style of the Congress. But, Aurobindo was also acutely aware that the Congress was still the only vehicle available for the propagation of his ideals and aims. It is this knowledge and the consequent frustration that he felt, which gives the 'New Lamps for Old' series the coruscating honesty, that can be felt even after the lapse of a century. By analysing and exposing the weaknesses of the Congress and its leadership, Aurobindo was clarifying, to himself and to his readers, how the Congress must change itself in order to effectively champion the cause of India. The Congress of these articles was the reverse of the Congress that Aurobindo and his allies wanted and would try to create.

Divine Shakti

If radical change was not to now come through the Congress, but only after a time when it would be transformed into a real weapon, what, then, was the way out? It would have to come through a violent revolution. The clandestinely published pamphlet *Bhawani Mandir* (Temple of Goddess Bhawani) outlined the organization and programme for revolutionary groups. Aurobindo said that the idea for the pamphlet was Barin's, and he had just written it. A close reading shows that Barin may have suggested that Aurobindo write it, but the ideas and content unquestionably came from the mind of Aurobindo.

Bhawani Mandir begins with the simple declaration that a temple dedicated to the Goddess Bhawani must be built upon a hill. But who is Bhawani? She is the infinite energy that emanates from the Eternal and manifests differently in different ages: 'In the present age, the Mother is manifested as the mother of Strength. She is pure Shakti.'[75] Aurobindo noted that Shakti was present in different forms across the world, and that India, too, needed to reawaken it. He said that previous attempts to do so had flickered and burnt out: 'Our beginnings are mighty, but they have neither sequel nor fruit.'[76] Aurobindo insisted that all attempts to revive industry and other aspects of economic life would fail without Shakti.

Aurobindo queries if it is the lack of bhakti which is holding India back:

> Bhakti is the living flame, Shakti is the fuel. If the fuel is scanty how long can the fire endure?' The conclusion is that Shakti is what is really required. Because India can be reborn only when it has Shakti: 'For what is a nation? It is a mighty Shakti, composed of the Shaktis off all the millions of units that make up the nation... the living unity of the Shakti of three hundred millions of people...'[77]

At the time that Aurobindo wrote *Bhawani Mandir*, he also wrote a poem in Sanskrit, 'Bhawani Bharati'. The poem was not published in his lifetime, having been spirited away by the police in Calcutta. It was recovered in 1985 and published in 1997. In tone and spirit, it echoes *Bhawani Mandir*. It strives to arouse the spirit of people across the country against the British. The twenty-fourth of its 99 verses should give pause to those who consider Aurobindo a propagandist of Hindu communalism:

> *You who adore the triple form of the one Lord,*
> *You, my Mohammedan sons,*

---

[75] *Complete Works of Sri Aurobindo: Volume 6: Bande Mataram — I–II*, Sri Aurobindo Ashram, 1997, p. 79.
[76] Ibid.
[77] Ibid.

Who worship Him in
His uniqueness: I, the Mother, call of you, for all
Are my children, Shake off your slumber! Oh, hear![78]

And hear they would. For, in the fragment on the Congress in 1902, Aurobindo had also made a prophecy:

> But behind & under cover of this failure & falling back there has been slowly & silently gathering another & vaster wave the first voices of which are now being heard, the crests of hose foam are just mounting here & there into view. Soon it will push aside or assimilate its broken forerunner, occupy the sea and the ride on surging and shouting to its predestined failure or triumph. By the succession of such waves shall our national life move forward to its great & inevitable goal.[79]

The culture of nationalism would then transform into the religion of nationalism.

---

[78]Sri Aurobindo, *Bhawani Bharathi*, Translated by Richard P. Hartz, Sri Aurobindo Society, 2003.

[79]*Complete Works of Sri Aurobindo: Volume 6: Bande Mataram—I-II*, Sri Aurobindo Ashram, 1997, p. 65.

Section II

The Prophet of Nationalism

4

Backing into the Limelight (1906–07)

When Aurobindo arrived in Calcutta in 1906, he had no aspirations for a leadership position in the storm swirling in Bengal, thanks to the short-sightedness of the viceroy, Lord Curzon. He wrote in a 1934 letter:

> I do not care about having my name in any blessed place. I was never ardent about fame even in my political days; I preferred to remain behind the curtain, push people without their knowing it and get things done. It was the confounded British Government that spoiled my game by prosecuting me and forcing me to become publicly known as a 'leader'.[80]

He similarly added in his 1948 note, 'he preferred to remain and act and even to lead from behind the scenes without his name being known in public; it was the Government's action in prosecuting him as editor of the Bande Mataram that forced him into public view.'[81] Despite Aurobindo's visits to Calcutta and

---

[80]Venet, Luc, *Sri Aurobindo and the Revolution of India*, Createspace Independent Publishing, 2017.
[81]*Complete Works of Sri Aurobindo: Volume 36. Autobiographical Notes and Other Writings of Historical Interest*, Sri Aurobindo Ashram, 1997, p. 47.

other parts of Bengal over the years, he was still known to only a few people, and he obviously preferred it that way.

What was the situation in Bengal at the moment that had so excited Aurobindo? The torpor and sullen watchfulness that Aurobindo had seen on previous visits was gone. The whole province was in turmoil following the actual partition of Bengal on 16 October 1905. The announcement had been made on 7 July, and had immediately evoked a strong reaction. Supposedly done for administrative efficiency, the actual target was the educated Hindu middle class, which was then the backbone of the Congress. Curzon had an irrational phobia for the Congress, considering this little group of loyalists to be harbringers of revolution. The partition effectively made the Bengali speakers a linguistic minority in West Bengal, where they were outnumbered by non-Bengalis. In the East, the Bengali Hindus became a religious minority, in an area dominated by Muslims.

A huge meeting was held in Calcutta on 7 August, where the slogan of boycott was raised. Inspired by the Irish, the tactic was Indianized and quickly came to be known as Swadeshi—of one's own nation. It was decided that goods of British manufacture, such as textiles and salt, to name a few, would not be purchased. Instead, their Indian counterparts or non-British goods only would be bought. In fact, at many places, a bonfire of British goods took place. Thus, this practical way of sustaining the local economy became a vivid symbol of nationalism.

But there was an even more potent symbol of nationalism out there—cries of 'Bande Mataram (Hail the Mother)' echoed across Bengal. A song from Bankim Chandra Chatterjee's novel *Anandamath*, it became the war cry of the anti-partition movement. The slogan was chanted by every anti-partition procession and became a bugbear for the authorities, who soon banned it.

Matters became worse when the authorities came down hard on students, the backbone of the movement. Several circulars were issued by the administration to crush the movement. The Carlyle Circular issued by the chief secretary of Bengal, R.W. Carlyle, banned the participation of students in the Swadeshi movement, and those disobeying the edict were to be severely punished. Hot on its heels came a circular from Pedler, the director of public instruction, to colleges in Calcutta. He queried why those students who participated in a Swadeshi demonstration at Harrison Road should not be expelled. Fuel was added to the fire with a circular from P.C. Lyon, the chief secretary of the new province of East Bengal. He banned the singing of 'Bande Mataram' and the congregating of students in the streets with instructions that the police should arrest anyone who was rude to an Englishman or a Muslim.

There were two responses to these edicts. The first was on 7 November at the coastal town of Barisal, where the local leaders were distributing Swadeshi leaflets when the newly minted governor of East Bengal, Bampfylde Fuller, arrived on the scene. He declared the distribution a seditious act and threatened to arrest all present. Afraid that the situation could spiral out of control, the Moderate leaders retreated.

The Barisal incident had two important consequences. Thousands of miles away in Baroda, Aurobindo wrote his first scorching article on the political events, albeit one that did not see the light of day, and whose first page is missing. It is interesting, nevertheless, as with clarity of thought and expression, Aurobindo set out his views, which underwent little change over the next few years. He was angered by the behaviour of the leaders, 'No Bengali can read the account of the interview between Mr Fuller and the Barisal leaders, without a blush of shame for himself and his nation.' He warned, 'Let the authorities remember this, that when a Government breaks the Law, by their very act the people are absolved of obeying the law.'[82] What could the Barisal leaders have done? Aurobindo answers:

> Surely they should have repelled the insults with a calm and simple dignity, or if that would not serve, with a self-assertion as haughty, if less violent than the self-assertion of the unmannerly official before them, and to the demand for the withdrawal of their appeal they should have returned a plain and quiet negative. And if as a result, Mr Fuller were immediately to send them to the prison, or the whipping post, or the gallows itself, what difference would that make to their duty as public men & national leaders?[83]

Aurobindo was advocating what he would soon call passive resistance. And for the first time, but not the last, Aurobindo described the events unfolding in Bengal as the 'new nationalism'.

The second consequence was to have an immediate and direct impact on Aurobindo himself. Aurobindo's arrival in Calcutta may have been sudden, but it had been brewing for some time. A prominent personality from Bengal, Raja Subodh Mallick, had come in touch with Aurobindo through C.C. Dutt, an ICS officer who was a member of Aurobindo's revolutionary groups in Bengal. They had discussed the possibility of Aurobindo shifting to new work in Bengal.

The opportunity arose after a number of meetings had taken place in Bengal, calling for an independent national education system. A meeting of the National Council of Education took place in Calcutta on 9 November, at which Mallick announced that he was ready to donate Rs. 1,00,000 for the purpose of establishing the Bengal National College. The unspoken condition for this

---

[82]*Complete Works of Sri Aurobindo: Volume 6: Bande Mataram — I–II*, Sri Aurobindo Ashram, 1997, p. 100.
[83]Ibid.

largesse was that Aurobindo would head the new institution, though at a much reduced salary.

Professor Ghose Again

Aurobindo joined the Bengal National College as its first principal on 15 August 1906. Aside from administrative work, he also taught English, French, German, Indian history and geography, English history, and political science. He also set the examination papers in these subjects. Fortunately, Aurobindo had a number of able assistants, such as the historian Radha Kumud Mukhopadhyay, Sakharam Deuskar and Satish Chandra Mukherjee to help shoulder the burden.

Aurobindo resigned from the college on 2 August 1907, just before he was indicted in the *Bande Mataram* sedition case. But the college was only a part of his work—politics and revolution were his bread and butter. Aurobindo gave a farewell speech at the college on 23 August in which he told the students in ringing tones:

> There are times in a nation's history when Providence places before it one work, one aim, to which everything else, however high and noble in itself, has to be sacrificed. Such a time has now arrived for our Motherland when nothing is dearer than her service, when everything else is to be directed to that end. If you will study, study for her sake; train yourselves body and mind and soul for her service.[84]

Yugantar

Barin had also come with Aurobindo to Calcutta. He suggested to Aurobindo that it was necessary for the revolutionary underground

---

[84]*Complete Works of Sri Aurobindo: Volume 7: Bande Mataram — I–II*, Sri Aurobindo Ashram, 1997, p. 655.

to have a medium to spread their ideas amongst the people, and it should be in Bengali. Aurobindo agreed, and Barin and a few comrades immediately set up a newspaper in Bengali, which they named *Yugantar* (New Age). As Sri Aurobindo recollected, 'At Barin's suggestion he agreed to the starting of a paper, Yugantar, which was to preach open revolt and the absolute denial of the British rule and include such items as a series of articles containing instructions for guerilla warfare.'[85] One wonders how the eagle eyes of the zealous censors missed such articles. The first issue came out in mid-March and was immediately a success. Within a year, it had touched a circulation of 10,000 copies. However, this commercial success did not translate into financial success, as the high-minded revolutionary-journalists had no head for finances.

When *Yugantar* was first prosecuted, after having been given an official warning to tone down its language, it was decided that as a matter of policy, no defence would be offered in court, as the paper refused to accept the legitimacy of a foreign government. The self-described editor, Bhupendranath Datta, a younger brother of Swami Vivekananda, told the court, in remarks drafted by Aurobindo: 'I have done what I considered my duty to my country...I do not wish to make any further statement or to take any part in the case.'[86] He was sentenced to a year's imprisonment for his defiance. The already high stock of *Yugantar* rose still higher in the eyes of the public.

Aurobindo wrote a number of articles for the paper, but only the one titled 'Our Political Ideal' has been positively identified as his. It may well be Aurobindo's earliest published Bengali article. It is, in some ways, a restatement of all that Aurobindo had written clandestinely, updated to include the

---

[85]*Complete Works of Sri Aurobindo: Volume 6: Bande Mataram — I–II*, Sri Aurobindo Ashram, 1997, p. 50.

[86]*Complete Works of Sri Aurobindo: Volume 7: Bande Mataram — I–II*, Sri Aurobindo Ashram, 1997, p. 613.

current situation. He first attacked the idea that the British had given any benefit to India:

> For a nation whose mind and body are dependent on others, railways, telegraph, electricity, municipalities, universities and National Congresses—all the discoveries of science and all things belonging to Western political life—are only toys. It is only what is obtained by one's own exertion, which is a right; the gift of others does not constitute a right. What Ripon has given today, Minto will takeaway tomorrow; at a thousand meetings and associations, we shall cry loudly saying 'Alas! Our toys are gone, what a great injustice!' Childishness is a main symptom of our present political life.[87]

He then attacked the slave mentality engendered by the British in so many words:

> We are slaves even if we get high posts; the Civilian, the Judge, the Municipal Commissioners, the Chairman of the District Board, the Syndicate of the University, the Member of the Legislative Council wear chains; all of them are laying on the stage wearing chains. But then we have become so low-mind that we do not feel ashamed to boast of those chains being made of gold or silver. Slavery has like a thick fog enveloped our entire life.[88]

Next, Aurobindo hurled a verbal grenade at his favorite bête noire, the Congress:

> Many people are proclaiming this in the name of the National Congress: 'The English officials are ruling the country well. We shall help them in the work of administration by annually informing them of the prayers of the Indians, and only by

---

[87]Sri Aurobindo Ashram Archives & Research, December 1991, pp. 243–47.
[88]Ibid.

that means will British administration be faultless.' But the officials do not accept this unasked for help, but rather set it naught by calling all this the slave's impudence and impertinence of unripe intelligence. Every year, the Congress appears uninvited before the officials with the objective of helping them, and at last comes back with a load of insult on its head.[89]

But he noted that change was on the wing:

What is heartening is that after dreaming for so long, we have now opened our eyes and begun to realise our abject condition. This subservience to others in every sphere is no longer tolerable. Throughout the country the idea is gradually spreading that, we must, by whatever means, win independence in our education, economy and political life. This is the hope of the future. This is the sign that we have awakened and will listen no more to the old lullabies. We will heed no obstacle and stop at no one's command. We will surely arise.[90]

Into the Fray

Aurobindo recognized that the Congress, despite his intense dislike for it, was still the best but not-so-ideal vehicle through which he could take his ideas forward. In the wake of the Bengal partition, he recognized that two different viewpoints dominated the party in Bengal—the Moderates and the Nationalists. Among the Loyalists, he very carefully differentiated between two variations: 'The Moderates are a hybrid species, emotionally Nationalist, intellectually Loyalist. It is owing to this double nature that their

[89]Ibid.
[90]Ibid.

delusions acquire an infinite power for mischief.'[91] Surendranath Banerjea, the Grand Old Man of Bengal politics, was the prime example. A leader of the Moderates, he was also an opponent of the partition, and thus a Nationalist, with a foot in both camps and trusted by neither.

The Nationalist or New Party section of the Congress was led by Bipin Chandra Pal, whom Aurobindo met at Subodh Mallick's house, where he himself lived. The two held similar views on political issues and had a healthy respect for each other. When the annual session of the Bengal Provincial Congress was held in April 1906, Aurobindo accompanied the Nationalist group. Ironically, the venue was Barisal, which had been in the eye of the storm only recently.

The conference began on 12 April, with a crowd of thousands in attendance. Chants of 'Bande Mataram' rang out. The head of police asked Surendranath Banerjea to stop the singing of a banned song. After consulting the other delegates, he refused to do so. The next day, a crowd of 5,000 accompanied their leaders shouting 'Bande Mataram'. The police let the front ranks, which included Aurobindo, through. They stopped the rest and attacked them mercilessly. The leaders rushed back, and Banerjea was arrested. The conference reconvened for a third day, attended by an even bigger crowd—6,000 strong. The police came and ordered the proceedings to stop. To avoid any violence, they were quickly brought to a close. Aurobindo may not have been happy with the decision, but he was certainly pleased with the defiance shown.

Bipin Chandra Pal had been invited to speak at similar rallies in East Bengal, and Aurobindo accompanied him. He was pleased to see that in an area where earlier there had been sullen silence, people thronged in thousands to listen to Bipin preach the gospel

---

[91] *Complete Works of Sri Aurobindo: Volume 6: Bande Mataram — I–II*, Sri Aurobindo Ashram, 1997, p. 358.

of new nationalism. Aurobindo was content to listen and observe, though his reticence may also have had something to do with his imperfect command of Bengali. When some people ventured to ask Aurobindo to speak, Bipin intervened: 'Assimilate what I tell you. If he speaks, he will speak with fire.'[92] Aurobindo may have thought that he was not in the limelight. Yet, slowly but assuredly, he was backing into it. His presence at the front ranks in Barisal and at the side of Bipin had been noted. A CID file had been opened on him.

Bande Mataram and the First Trial

After his exhilarating tour of Bengal, Bipin Chandra Pal came to the conclusion that it was necessary for the Nationalist group to have a newspaper in English aligned with its viewpoint, as the Moderates had strong support among English-language papers. He named it *Bande Mataram* and asked Aurobindo to contribute to it, which he readily agreed to do. Aurobindo, after all, was a very unusual revolutionary. He never used a gun but always wielded a pen.

Bande Mataram was, to put it mildly, the most radical paper to have been published in India at the time. Only *Yugantar* could give it competition in that department. No other paper in the land had hit out at the British as the *Bande Matram* had in its lifetime. All the articles were published anonymously, and Aurobindo had put in place a team whose writings could not be distinguished from that of the other.

Bande Matram created a sensation. The Indian language papers were thrilled, and many of them reproduced articles in different languages in different parts of the country. The reputation

---

[92]Venet, Luc, *Sri Aurobindo and the Revolution of India*, Createspace Independent Publishing, 2017, p. 111.

of the paper reached as far as London, where the venerable *Times* referred more than once to its articles. The British bureaucracy and the pro-British English papers were apocalyptic.

When Aurobindo fell seriously ill and was unable to attend to the running of the paper, sharp differences surfaced between Bipin and the others. While the others were sympathetic to the revolutinary cause, Bipin was opposed to the use of any violence. Matters came to a head quickly, and Bipin was forced to leave, his name taken off the masthead. Aurobindo's name was put up but removed quickly at his instance. Yet, the mutual respect that Aurobindo and Bipin had for each other never waned after the break. Years later, Bipin wrote admiringly and perceptively about Aurobindo:

> The youngest in age among those who stand in the forefront of the Nationalist propaganda in India but in endowement, education, and character, perhaps, superior to them all— Aravinda seems distinctly marked out by Providence to play in the future of this movement a part not given to any of his colleagues and contemporaries. The other leaders of the movement have left their life behind them. Aravinda has his before him. Nationalism is their last love: it is Aravinda's first passion.[93]

Aurobindo and his co-writers were clear in their approach— they never attacked the English as a people or personally but pointed out the incongruity of the Raj and its true face, with administrative inefficiency, apathy and a lacksadical approach that aggravated famine and poverty. They became very good at writing close to the edge but never crossed the line into what was called sedition.

---

[93]Cited in: Banerjee, Anurag (ed.), *Sri Aurobindo: His Political Life and Activities*, Overman Foundation, 2012.

Aurobindo made plain his ultimate aim in one of his first editorials: 'The issue has been fairly put between the Indian people and the alien bureaucracy. "Destroy or thou shalt be destroyed", and the issue will have to be fought out, not "it may be a century hence", but now, in the next two or three decades.' Again and again, he ripped into the Congress:

> The true policy of the Congress movement should have been from the beginning to gather together under its flag all the elements of strength that exist in this huge country. The Brahmin Pandit and the Mahommedean Maulvi, the caste organizations and the trade unions, the labourer and the artisan, the coolie at his work and the peasant in his field, none of these should have been left out of the sphere of our activities.[94]

When communal frenzy overtook East Bengal, Aurobindo did not stigmatize the Muslim community but castigated the administration as the real culprit: 'It is part of the policy also to attack it by localities even in the affected areas and not as a whole, to destroy it before the defence has organised itself, and to use as instruments the Salimullah sect of Mahomedans, while the Police confine themselves to keeping the ring.'[95]

After the prosecution of *Yugantar*, it was certain that it would only be a matter of time before the turn of *Bande Mataram* came. The files of the paper were quickly scoured for any reference to Aurobindo, which were cut out with a knife to erase any possibility of evidence against him. The police raided the premises on 7 June 1907 with a search warrant to look for evidence against Aurobindo being the editor but failed to find it. They also had an

---

[94] *Complete Works of Sri Aurobindo: Volume 6: Bande Mataram — I–II*, Sri Aurobindo Ashram, 1997, p. 126.
[95] Ibid. 259

arrest warrant for him. On hearing of it, Aurobindo immediately surrendered and was given bail.

The entire prosecution was a fiasco. Bipin Chandra Pal was called in to name Aurobindo as the editor. He refused to do so and was sentenced to six months in prison for contempt. There was not a shred of evidence to confirm that Aurobindo was the editor. The exasperated prosecutor shouted in court that he did not care whether Aurobindo was the editor or not, but he was certainly the brain behind the newspaper. The paper had reprinted an article from *Yugantar* in translation, which was deemed seditious. The printer was imprisoned. Aurobindo was set free for lack of evidence. The judge, Kingsford, noted that Aurobindo was 'a man of exceptionally good attainments who had differentiated himself from the ordinary staff by refusing to take any fixed salary for his labours.'[96]

When Aurobindo was arrested, he was barely known in Calcutta, and that too only among a few. By the time the *Bande Matram* trial ended, he was a national figure. Poet Rabindranath Tagore, an old family friend, welcomed his release with a poem:

> *Rabindranath, O Aurobindo, bows to thee! O friend, my*
> *Country's friend, O Voice incarnate, free, of India's soul...*
> *The fiery messenger that with the lamp of God hath come.*
> *...Rabindranath, O Aurobindo, bows to thee.*

Bande Mataram continued publishing apace until it began to lose force and became an unviable financial proposition during Aurobindo's incarceration in Alipore Jail. Rather than shut down voluntarily, it was decided that the government should be forced to stop its publication. How? By running highly charged articles that would leave the administration with no option but to shut it

---

[96]Venet, Luc, *Sri Aurobindo and the Revolution of India*, Createspace Independent Publishing, 2017, p. 149.

down. The *Bande Mataram* thus ended, not with a whimper but in a blaze of glory. Sri Aurobindo later wrote of *Bande Mataram* with justifiable pride: 'The *Bande Mataram* was unique in journalistic history in the influence that it exercised in converting the mind of a people and preparing it for revolution.'[97]

The Nationalist Leader

Aurobindo may have preferred to fade into obscurity and work from behind the scenes, but fate was against him. In the absence of Bipin Chandra Pal, who was in jail, he had to take a leading role in the Nationalist or Extremist (as their opponents called them) camp of the Congress. Aurobindo was now openly and avowedly a political leader.

Earlier, in 1906, the Calcutta session of the Congress had seen a bitter fight between the Moderates and the Extremists. Bal Gangadhar Tilak, however, had been able to have the general assembly approve of his proposals on boycott, national education and swadeshi, to the dismay of the Moderates. But the icing on the cake had been delivered by the president, Dadabhai Naoroji, who had declared that swaraj (an ambigious word—depending on who used it, it could mean autonomy or independence) was the policy of the Congress. Aurobindo appreciated the irony that the first use of swaraj on the Congress platform had been by a legendary Moderate.

Now, the first order of the day was to lead the Extremist faction at Midnapore, where the Moderates had the numbers and refused to accept amendments moved by the Extremists. The session broke up in chaos, with lathis being wielded freely by all comers. Incredibly, the Moderate leadership had the police and

[97]*Complete Works of Sri Aurobindo: Volume 36: Autobiographical Notes and Other Writings of Historical Interest*, Sri Aurobindo Ashram, 1997, p. 56.

magistrate on call in fear of possible violence. The police waded in with abandon. The stage was supposed to shift to Nagpur, where the Extremists were strong and could dominate the Congress session slated to take place there. The Moderates managed to have it shifted to Surat, where they had a majority.

The evening before he left for Surat, Aurobindo had a visitor. It was Henry Nevinson, the correspondent for the *Manchester Guardian*. Nevinson saw before him 'a youngish man... intent dark eyes looked from his thin, clear-cut face with a gravity that seemed immovable, but the figure and bearing were those of an English graduate'.[98] Aurobindo explained to him that the Extremists planned to keep themselves totally aloof of the government and its institutions. Nevinson's impression was that Aurobindo was a dreamer, but one who would ensure his dream came true. And the dream was to turn Congress into a vehicle for freedom.

Aurobindo was now a national figure and had made public appearances and given speeches. This new-found fame showed in the progress of his train to Surat. Barin records the extraordinary scenes: 'Aurobindo the new idol of the nation was hardly known then by his face, and at every small and big station a frantic crowd rushed about in the station platform looking for him in the first and second class carriages, while all the time Aurobindo sat unobserved in a third class compartment.'[99]

---

[98]Nevinson, Henry W., *The New Spirit in India*, Harper and Brothers, 1908, p. 226.
[99]Ghose, Barin, *Sri Aurobindo (as I understand him)*, unpublished manuscript, Sri Aurobindo Archives.

5

Stormy Surat, Imperial Backlash (1907–08)

Aurobindo's journey to placid Surat, the venue of what would be the most consequential session in the history of the Indian National Congress to date, was eventful, especially by the standards of the time. There were large, excited crowds waiting to catch a glimpse of him, a phenomenon not to be seen again till the advent of Gandhi on the national scene. Aurobindo left Calcutta on 21 December 1907. The next day, he gave a speech at Nagpur and Amravati.

When Aurobindo reached Bombay on 23 December, he gave a speech on the beach. Barin recalled:

> We detrained in Bombay, there a meeting was arranged on the sea beach. We could hardly walk to the place through the living streams converging through the streets and lanes towards the chosen spot, automatically stopping all vehicular traffic for a time. It was a sight for the Gods to see: the awakening of a whole nation from its age-long sleep and inertia into conscious life of flaming aspiration.[100]

---

[100]Ibid.

High Noon

When they finally reached Surat, they found a city agog in anticipation of the upcoming battle between the Moderates and the Extremists. The Moderate leader Pherozshah Mehta sent Gopal Krishna Gokhale, the most eminent of the Moderates, to Surat to ensure that the locals were on their side. Gokhale was also made the chief of the Reception Committee. What was it that the Extremists wanted? A reiteration of the four resolutions they had managed to push through at Calcutta—swaraj, boycott, swadeshi and national education.

Whatever misgivings the Extremists had about the intentions of the Moderates were confirmed when they discovered that none of their topics—boycott, swadeshi and swaraj—were listed for discussion at the session. Then, they discovered that an amendment was to be made to the Congress Constitution in which, negating Calcutta, swaraj was defined as being self-government, similar to other members of the British Empire. This had to be subscribed to by all members. Moreover, the resolution on Swadeshi was to be amended so that it was boycott of foreign goods alone and not foreign institutions. The Moderates wanted the words 'on National lines and National control' to be replaced by 'an independent system'.

An outraged Tilak gave a ferocious speech against the changes and omissions. A report from the Bombay Presidency Police noted the Extremists reaction:

> The first meeting of the Nationalists' Conference was held on the 24th December... Mr Ghose, being elected to the chair, observed that the object of the conference was to disseminate the gospel of Nationalism... It was the object of the Conference to enforce the views of the Nationalists on the Indian National Congress an to make the Congress,

which had hitherto been a body for the concentration of opinion, a body for the concentration of work.[101]

The Nationalists made futile attempts to reach a compromise with the Moderates, the biggest being the decision not to insist on Lala Lajpat Rai, the Punjab Congress leader who had just returned from exile in Burma, as the president, but were rebuffed.

On the first day of the conference, there were cheers and cries of shame when Lajpat Rai entered the pavilion. When the President-designate, Rash Behari Ghosh, accompanied by Moderate leaders, entered, there was an immediate tumult. Pherozshah Mehta proposed Ghosh's name, and Surendranath Banerjea tried to second it. He was drowned by the noise, which forced the session to be suspended. Aurobindo turned to Tilak and said: 'Mr Tilak, you had no confidence so far. But this is the nation. Look at it. From today, it is the only power in India.'[102]

The next day, Tilak gave a note to Tribhuvandas Malvi, the chairman of the session, saying that he wanted to move a resolution on the presidential election. After speeches by Banerjea and Motilal Nehru, his reminders being ignored, Tilak marched to the stage. Ghosh, rising to take the presidential chair, paused. Malvi asked Tilak what the matter was. Tilak said he wanted to move a resolution. Ghosh insisted he had been elected. Tilak retorted that he had not. Noise arose, with slogans and counter-slogans being shouted. Aurobindo gave a signal to his supporters to bring matters to a head. Suddenly, a Mahratha shoe hit Mehta and then Banerjea. Pandemonium reigned. The leaders of both factions were taken out by their supporters. Lajpat Rai tried again for a compromise and failed yet again. This led to a split in the Congress.

Lala Lajpat Rai later went to Tilak and said that the government would now come down hard on the Extremists. Tilak agreed and

---

[101]Hiranmayi, *Sri Aurobindo in Surat*, Sri Aurobindo Society, Surat, 2007, p. 42.
[102]Ibid.

said the country would not withstand such repression, and wanted to sign the new Congress Constitution and keep the party intact. Aurobindo and a few others disagreed. They believed that the Moderates would wither away, and the Extremist faction would get the backing of the people. In the short term, Tilak proved right. Sri Aurobindo on the other hand,

> had hoped that the country would be strong enough to face the repression…; but he also thought that even if there was a temporary collapse the repression would create a deep change in the hearts and minds of the people and the whole nation would swing over to nationalism and the ideal of independence. This actually happened and when Tilak returned from jail in Burma after 6 years he was able, in conjunction with Mrs Besant not only to revive the Congress but to make it representative of a nation pledged to the nationalist cause.[103]

In the long term, Aurobindo proved right. The events of Surat ensured the advent of Gandhi.

Inner Ascendance, Outer Ascendancy

After the dramatic end of the Surat session, with Congress unity in tatters, Aurobindo was invited to speak at various places across the Deccan. But first, he crossed the border into his old home, Baroda, on 1 January 1908. The returning hero was received with a roar of acclaim. Crowds followed him everywhere. Aurobindo spoke at a packed public meeting and met his old employer, the Maharaja.

While Aurobindo was ensconced at the house of his old friend Jadhav, Barin brought to him an unusual visitor, Vishnu Bhaskar

---

[103]*Complete Works of Sri Aurobindo: Volume 36: Autobiographical Notes and Other Writings of Historical Interest*, Sri Aurobindo Ashram, 1997, p. 83.

Lele, a civil servant by profession. Barin had come across Lele while he was on the lookout for a spiritual instructor for a band of revolutionaries that he was trying to create. Lele had great experience in yoga. Barin, impressed by his positive experiences with Lele, brought him to meet his brother. Aurobindo had been having trouble with his yogic experiences recently. Due to his strenuous political and journalistic activity, Aurobindo had fallen ill in 1906. He found little time to practise pranayama, and as a result, his new-found energy had disappeared.

After he explained it all to Lele, he was taken away to another house for a few days. Lele told him that there was no need to give up his public life and gave him some advice. Sri Aurobindo noted that he was instructed thus:

> Look and you will see that your thoughts come to you from outside. Before they enter, fling them back'. I sat down and looked and saw to my astonishment that it was so; I saw and felt concretely the thought approaching as if to enter through or above the head and was able to push it back concretely before it came inside. From that moment, in principle, the mental being in me became a free Intelligence, a universal Mind, not limited to the narrow circle of personal thought or a labourer in a thought-factory, but a receiver of knowledge from all the hundred realms of being and free too to chose what it willed in this vast sight-empire and thought-empire.[104]

Lele did not want Aurobindo to immediately engage in political activity, but he had no choice. In the wake of Surat, the Extremists needed to bolster their position. With that in mind, Aurobindo was asked to speak at a number of places in Maharashtra. After speeches in Poona and Girgaon, a part of Bombay, he had to speak

---

[104]Ibid. 109.

in Bombay on 9 January 1908. He confessed to Lele that he had no idea of what to say. Lele told him not to worry and to just greet the Divine in the audience with the traditional namaskar, and what he had to say would come to him. And that was exactly what happened. It was possibly his greatest speech, and for some, his most controversial, as he equated God and nationalism, which has been construed as a Hindu communal appeal, a question we shall revert to later.

Aurobindo did as instructed and found the words pouring out of a silent mind. In his quiet, clear voice, he declared:

> What is Nationalism? Nationalism is not a mere political programme; Nationalism is a religion that has come from God; Nationalism is a creed in which you shall have to live. Let noo man dare to call himself a Nationalist if he does so merely with intellectual pride, thinking that he is more patriotic, thinking that he is something higher than those who do not call themselves by that name. If you are going to be a Nationalist, if you are going to assent to this religion of Nationalism, you must do it in the religious spirit. You must remember that you are the instrument of God for the salvation of your own country. You must live as the instruments of God.[105]

Aurobindo then proceeded to speak at several other cities, where his speeches were received with great admiration, before returning to Calcutta. Lele advised him that he should always listen to the voice of the Divine, then he would not need anything else. It was to turn out to be a very fruitful piece of advice.

Back in Calcutta, Aurobindo returned to writing and politics, thoroughly re-energized, thanks to Lele's intervention. Realizing

---

[105]*Complete Works of Sri Aurobindo: Volume 7: Bande Mataram — I–II*, Sri Aurobindo Ashram, 1997, p. 818.

that dark days were looming for the nationalist movement, with the Congress split down the middle, Aurobindo warned:

> The times are thickening already with the shadow of a great darkness. The destruction of the Congress, begun at Surat, is the prelude for the outburst of the storm that has long been brewing. Great issues were involved in that historic struggle at Surat of which none of the actors were aware... The fair hopes of an orderly and peaceful evolution of self-government, which the first energies of the new movement had fostered, are gone for ever. Revolution, bare and grim, is preparing her battlefield... We could have wished it otherwise, but God's will be done.[106]

Aurobindo, however, was clear about the trajectory that the nationalist movement must take—and which it did take, setting the stage for the advent of the Gandhian era:

> We should be absolutely unsparing in our attack on whatever obstructs the growth of the nation, and never be afraid to call a spade a spade... Open attack, unsparing criticism, the severest satire, the most wounding irony, are all methods perfectly justifiable and indispensable in politics. We have strong things to say; let us say them strongly; we have stern things to do; let us do them sternly.' Then, Aurobindo delivered an interesting warning: 'But there is always a danger of strength degenerating into violence and sternness into ferocity, and that should be avoided so far as it is humanly possible.[107]

Aurobindo, who had been at the forefront of the battle that divided the Congress at Surat, tried to maintain the unity of the party at the

---

[106]Ibid. 1072.

[107]*Complete Works of Sri Aurobindo: Volume 6: Bande Mataram — I–II*, Sri Aurobindo Ashram, 1997, p. 309.

provincial level in Bengal. For Aurobindo understood clearly that a split there would weaken the nationalist movement nationally, possibly even decisively. Steam began to build up on both sides when it came to the choice of the person to preside over the annual session to be held at Pabna. Both sides wanted to see their nominee in charge. The tension was defused when Rabindranath Tagore, universally respected, with Aurobindo's support, offered to chair the session himself. The offer was accepted with alacrity, and the session went off without a hitch. All the resolutions were passed without a debate, and in favour of the Extremists. Aurobindo wrote the very next day about Tagore at the helm of the conference: 'Out of the gladness of his heart there burst from him a flood of inspiring eloquence which made the whole audience astir with feelings of impassioned aspiration. Swaraj was the theme of his eloquence and to anyone listening carefully it was evident that Swaraj unlimited and without reservation, was the ideal enshrined in the heart of the poet.'[108]

The unity was, however, short-lived.

Around this time, one day, Abinash Bhattacharya, Aurobindo's secretary and man of all jobs, noticed that his diet had changed and had become lighter. This was the result of the arrival of Lele and a companion. Lele led the family in fasting, and visiting places of worship such as Kalighat and Sri Ramakrishna's Belur Math. When Lele asked Aurobindo whether he had adhered to the advice given earlier, Aurobindo told him that he had stopped the practice of meditation, as meditation was going on within constantly. Lele misunderstood, and told Aurobindo that the devil had entered him. Soon after, not only did their ways part, their idea of yoga, too, began to diverge.

---

[108]*Complete Works of Sri Aurobindo: Volume 7: Bande Mataram — I–II*, Sri Aurobindo Ashram, 1997, p. 873.

Meanwhile, Barin...

Barin appears to have been trying his level best to bring about the crisis in the nationalist movement predicted by his brother. He continued to pursue his role as an incendiary journalist with *Yugantar* and his revolutionary work. Aurobindo's links with these revolutionary groups slackened and took less of his time as he became more and more preoccupied with *Bande Mataram* and open political activity. Barin's involvement, on the other hand, continued apace. Barin was keen to pursue his old idea of a group of religiously inclined revolutionaries.

Barin and his comrades were determined to kill Fuller, the governor of East Bengal. Learning that he would be coming to Calcutta by train, they waited outside the city at a certain point. They would board the train and kill Fuller. The train never came, and the group trudged back to Calcutta, where they sheepishly told Aurobindo of their misadventure. He quietly told them to go home.

Fired by his old dream of a revolutionary ashram, Barin decided to create it at Maniktola, a suburb of Calcutta where the Ghose brothers had inherited a dilapidated garden-house. Barin set up shop here. The day began at four in the morning. The group studied the Bhagvad Gita, the Upanishads, the recent Russia–Japan war, and carried out strenuous physical exercises and practised with weapons. Soon, Barin managed to put together a bomb factory too. The group grew in numbers, with the lead being taken by Nolini Kanta Gupta (who was to become close to Sri Aurbindo), Ullaskar Dutt and Praful.

When Lele arrived he understood what the true nature of Barin's group was. He told them that their objective, the liberation of India, was commendable, but it should take place in a peaceful manner. He added that violence was incompatible with yoga. Yoga, he told them, meant a cleansing of the heart. Unfazed, they laughed at him.

The first attempts at making bombs failed, but soon they

succeeded. When a bomb blew up mid-air, it killed Praful, who was standing quite near it. They also decided to dynamite trains, but the triggers failed, and the trains sped away safely. Finally, in December 1908, the dynamite actually exploded. It lifted the train carrying Andrew Fraser, the newly appointed governor of East Bengal, off the rails and into the air—after which the train crashed down but did not derail. The governor got off to inspect the damage and ordered an investigation.

Barin's pyrotechnically challenged band of bombers then changed tack. They decided to attack officials of the Raj who showed a particular brutality while cracking down on the nationalists in Bengal. They settled on a judge, Douglas Kingsford—the very same man who had acquitted Aurobindo in the *Bande Mataram* case. Kingsford was known for the harsh sentences he handed out to journalists who had the temerity to take on the might of the Raj. He also ordered the severe public flogging of students who had been arrested for shouting 'Bande Matram'. He was, clearly, a prime target.

The first attempt to kill Kingsford was with a book bomb. A bomb was placed within a heavy legal volume and delivered to Kingsford's house by a member of the group. However, the ever-busy judge did not get the time to glance through the book, which probably saved his life.

Thanks to the innumerable threats to Kingsford's life, he was transferred to Muzaffarpur, with four policemen charged with his protection. However, unknown to Barin, the Maniktola group had been identified by the police and was put under surveillance. Aurobindo and Barin were under constant watch.

Barin decided to take action against Kingsford and sent two men for the purpose—Khudiram Bose and Prafulla Chaki. On 29 April, they followed Kingsford and then stationed themselves at the gate of the club, where Kingsford and his wife were playing cards. When they finished playing, they got into the second of two identical coaches. The wife and daughter of Pringle Kennedy, a local lawyer, got into the first one. The two waiting men had been seen being accosted by two policemen, who let them off. Seeing the coach appear, they assumed it was Kingsford and hurled a bomb inside. Both occupants were killed instantly. Khudiram and Prafulla took off in opposite directions. Overpowered, Prafulla escaped and shot himself with his own pistol. Khudiram was held at the station, tried and executed.

The Empire Strikes Back

Aurobindo was sitting at his desk at the office of the *Bande Matram* on 1 May when fellow journalist Shyam Sundar Chakravarty handed him a telegram, which informed him of the Muzaffarpur killings. He also came across a Calcutta news report in which the police commissioner of Calcutta announced that the identity of the perpetrators was known and they would soon be caught.

He immediately sent a message to Barin to remove all weapons and destroy all documents. Barin and his men got down to the task. They hid the weapons and burnt papers and lay down to rest. They planned to get up early and escape. The police woke them up. They were made to stand in a line all day and then taken to Lal Bazar police station.

Aurobindo went home and was woken up at 5 a.m. on 2 May by the shouting of Sarojini. Armed policemen entered his room and surrounded him. The terrified Mrinalini ran out of the room. Superintendent Cregan, after confirming his identity, arrested him. Aurobindo asked to see the warrant and realized that it was only for a search of the premises and not to arrest him. In short, his arrest was illegal. However, he knew that it would be futile to protest and complied. He was handcuffed, and a rope tied around his waist, though it was removed later. He was taken to Lal Bazar and then to a police station on Royal Street. Abinash Bhattacharya and Sailen Bose had also been arrested at the house.

The next morning, Aurobindo was taken back to Lal Bazar, where he was put in solitary confinement. He was interrogated time and again, and he concluded that the officers wanted to connect him to Barin's group. On 5 May, he was taken to the court of the examining magistrate, where he met a lawyer and a relative. The lawyer told him that the police claimed to have found incriminating evidence at his house. Aurobindo told the relative that he would be proved innocent. Sri Aurobindo wrote, 'From that moment on I had a firm belief that it would be so. In the beginning, during solitary imprisonment, the mind was a little uneasy. But after three days of prayer and meditation an unshakeable peace and faith again overwhelmed the being.'[109]

In the meantime, unknown to Aurobindo, Barin, under the impression that he could save his elder brother and the others from punishment by taking everything on himself, led the police to the hidden weapons cache and other documents. Aurobindo was stunned when he later heard of Barin's incredible act, which, rather than helping, probably put everybody in further jeopardy.

The court ordered the imprisonment of Aurobindo at the Alipore Jail. Sri Aurobindo later recalled this episode as a turning point in his life:

> I did not know that day would mean the end of a chapter of my life, and that stretched before me a year's imprisonment during which period all my human relations would cease, that for a whole year I would have to live, beyond the pale of society, like an animal in a cage. And when I could re-enter the world of activity, it would not be the old familiar Aurobindo Ghosh. Rather it would be a new being, a new character, intellect, life, mind, embarking upon a new course of action that would come out of the ashram at Alipore.[110]

---

[109]Sri Aurobindo, *Tales of Prison Life*, Sri Aurobindo Ashram, 1974.
[110]Ibid.

6

Sadhana at Alipore Ashram (1908–09)

Aurobindo entered Alipore Jail on 5 May 1908 and was released on 6 May 1909. This year-long incarceration proved to be a turning point in his life. The spiritual catharsis that he underwent during this time was, in some ways, the foundation upon which the superstructure of Integral Yoga of Sri Aurobindo was later built. The experiences that Aurobindo had in jail exposed him to the possibilities and potential that actually exist in the spiritual realm. In the political sphere, these experiences brought about a sharpening of his ideas as well as a distancing.

Sri Aurobindo wrote a lengthy autobiographical essay, albeit incomplete, which was published as *Karakahani* (Prison Tales). It is our primary source for the events that took place within and without during this time. Its blunt honesty, leavened by a style that deployed irony as the seasoning of choice, so familiar to readers of *Bande Mataram*, makes it a powerful and refreshing document. Interestingly, it is probably the only autobiographical writing (outside of conversations) of his in which he does not speak of himself in the third person. This possibly may have been due to the starkness of what he was writing about.

Prison Life

Aurobindo walked into a cell that was about nine feet by five feet. There were no windows; and iron bars at the entry, which opened into a small courtyard with a door. This had a small hole through which the guard could peep into the cell. Prison life was harsh. The only possessions the prisoners had was a plate, a tin cup and a bowl. Of the bowl he wrote:

> The bowl was free from all caste restrictions, beyond discrimination: in the prison cell it helped in the act of ablution; later with the same bowl I gargled, bathed; a little later when I had to take my food, the lentil soup or vegetable soup was poured into the same container, I drank water out of it and washed my mouth.[111]

The humiliation of such a situation knocked out the stuffing of any arrogance or disgust. It forced on one the virtue of acceptance of whatever came one's way.

The food that was given daily was the same, which consisted of dirty coarse rice, watery lentil soup and vegetables mixed with grass and leaves. The summer months that he spent in the cell were perhaps the worst part of his stay in jail, for there was no way to get protection from the heat. At night, there were two sheets for sleeping arrangements, with one sheet serving as a pillow. It was perhaps a good thing that Aurobindo had grown up leading a spartan lifestyle, for it provided him with the strength to withstand the blows that would have felled any ordinary person. Aurobindo was also lucky in the treatment that he was given by the doctors who oversaw the prison inmates. Humane, they did their best for the prisoners. In fact, one of them tried to get Aurobindo to stay a little longer in his hospital bed during an

---

[111]Ibid.

illness, as it would help him. Besides the doctors' friendliness, Aurobindo was also asked by one of his guards if he wanted to send a message to his family. He was also shown small gestures of humanity by various people in the jail, which greatly moved him.

The Spiritual Adventurer

In his legendary speech at Uttarpara, made not too long after his release, and thus closer in time to the events it described, Aurobindo vividly spoke of the great anguish that he had felt during his arrest and subsequent imprisonment. It deeply affected his usual equanimity and threatened his spiritual balance. Aurobindo said:

> When I was arrested and hurried to the Lal Bazar Hajat, I was shaken in faith for a while, for I could not look into the heart of His intention. Therefore I faltered for a moment and cried out in my heart to Him, 'What is this that has happened to me? I believed that I had a mission to work for the people of my country and until that work was done, I should have Thy protection. Why then am I here and on such a charge?'[112]

Aurobindo had been leading a frenetic life, without even a minute free. Now, suddenly, time hung heavy on his hands. He tried to meditate:

> In this solitary prison, not having anything else to do, I tried to meditate for a longer period. But for those unaccustomed, it is not easy to control and steady the mind pulled in a thousand directions. Somehow I was able to concentrate for an hour and a half or two, later the mind rebelled while the body too was fatigued. At first, the mind was full of thoughts

---

[112]*Complete Works of Sri Aurobindo: Volume 8: Karmayogin,* Sri Aurobindo Ashram, 1997, p. 3.

of many kinds. Afterwards devoid of human conversation and an insufferable listlessness due to the absence of any subject of thought the mind gradually grew devoid of the capacity to think.[113]

The boredom of prison life had seeped deep within him. He found himself unable to focus, and one day, there was a whirlwind of thoughts in his mind. Alarmed, he offered a prayer: 'Then I called upon God with eagerness and intensity and prayed to him to prevent my loss of intelligence. That very moment there spread over my being such a gentle and cooling breeze, the heated brain became relaxed, easy and supremely blissful such as in all my life I had never known before.'

Aurobindo realized that the Divine had been playing with him, trying to get him to see how weak his mind actually was so that he could make it stronger. Sri Aurobindo understood that 'It was to reveal and expose before my mind its own weakness so that I might get rid of it forever. For one who seeks the yogic state, crowd and solitude should mean the same. Indeed, the weakness dropped off within very few days...'

After a few days in prison, he was permitted to receive books from home– the Upanishads and the Bhagavad Gita—but he was now convinced that even without their aid, he was strong enough to withstand any pressure. At this time, he also became aware of the power and effectiveness of prayer. Thanks to the intervention of the prison doctor and the vice-director of the prison, he was given permission to take regular long walks outside. This he did with a vengeance, walking up to two hours at a time while reciting from the Upanishads. Gradually, he found that his perception of reality was changing. He began to see God in everything, animate and inanimate. All the trees, birds and animals seemed to him to be simply aspects of God. He wrote:

---

[113]Sri Aurobindo, *Tales of Prison Life*, Sri Aurobindo Ashram, 1974.

As I went on doing like this, sometimes the prison ceased to be a prison at all. The high wall, those iron bars, the white wall, the green-leaved tree shining in sunlight—it seemed as if these common-place objects were not unconscious at all, but they were vibrating with a universal consciousness, they loved me and wished to embrace me, or so I felt. Once in a while, it seemed as if God Himself was standing under the tree, playing upon his Flute of Delight and, with his sheer charm, drawing my very soul out... The hard cover of my life opened up and a spring of love for all creatures gushed from within.[114]

This vision of Krishna was to remain with Aurobindo. It is interesting that Krishna is the only Puranic god to be mentioned by him as an inspiration. He longed to have a vision of Krishna again, and it was repeated several times. In the Uttarpara speech, he reported what Krishna said to him:

When you were cast into jail, did not your heart fail and did you not cry out to me, where is Thy protection? Look now at the Magistrate, look now at the Prosecuting Counsel. I looked and it was not the Magistrate whom I saw, it was Vasudeva, it was Narayana who was sitting there on the bench. I looked at Prosecuting Counsel and it was not the Counsel for the prosecution that I saw; it was Sri Krishna who sat there, it was my Lover and Friend who sat there and smiled.[115]

During the preliminary trial, all the prisoners were brought together and kept in the same dock in the courtroom. Sri Aurobindo noted wryly, 'I found that while spending one's time in solitary imprisonment had grown easy and pleasant, it was

---

[114]Ibid.
[115]Ibid.

not that easy in the midst of the crowd and in the life-and-death game of a serious political case.'[116]

At one point he found himself levitating. Sri Aurobindo said: 'One part of my body was slightly in contact with the ground and the rest was raised up against the wall and I know I could not have held up my body like that normally even if I had wanted to. I also found that the body remained suspended like that without any exertion on my part.'[117]

On another occasion, he had an encounter with Swami Vivekananda:

> It is a fact that I was hearing constantly the voice of Vivekananda speaking to me for a fortnight in the jail in my solitary meditation and felt his presence... The voice spoke only on a special and limited but very important field of spiritual experience and it ceased as soon as it had finished saying all that had to be said on that subject.[118]

Such new experiences within led to the broadening of his consciousness, and Aurobindo also gained an understanding of matters that had previously been in the background such as art and architecture. These would manifest in articles that he would write upon his release.

The Trial

According to British jurisprudence, an initial preliminary trial had to be held in order to ascertain that the evidence was strong enough to prove the charges laid against the accused. The preliminary trial in the Alipore Bomb Case began on 8 May 1908.

---

[116]Ibid.
[117]Ibid.
[118]Ibid.

The accused—singing, laughing, joking—were brought to the Alipore courts from the jail and sent back there at the end of the day's proceedings.

Interestingly, just as the trial was under way, unknown to anyone outside a charmed circle, an intense debate was going on between high officials on what should be done with Aurobindo. These documents make for fascinating reading and indicate the level of interest the Raj took in the welfare of Aurobindo. The British believed Aurobindo to be one of the top leaders of the nationalist cause, and their interest pointed to the level of influence they believed he wielded in the movement.

On the one hand, there was a group worried as to whether there was enough evidence to convict Aurobindo. Reflective of this viewpoint was this letter from the chief secretary of Bengal to the home secretary:

> The conviction of the other persons concerned would be of no avail if Arabinda were set free; for, in that case he would lose no time in starting a fresh conspiracy, and the work now done would be altogether in vain... In the interest of peace and good government, it is absolutely necessary that this man should be removed from the political arena.[119]

Then, there was the view enunciated by Governor Andrew Fraser in a letter to the viceroy, Lord Minto:

> The man is able, cunning, fanatical. He is the leader. He has been in the forefront of all, advising seditious writing and authorizing murder. But he has kept himself, like a careful and valued General, out of sight of the enemy. We cannot get evidence against him, such as would secure his conviction in a Court. But we have been fortunate enough to get papers which

---

[119]Das, Manoj, *Sri Aurobindo in the First Decade of the 20th Century*, Sri Aurobindo Ashram, 2003.

show his connection with the conspiracy, quite sufficient to convince the reasonable mind and justify deportation. I certainly hope no sentiments will be allowed to prevent this.[120]

The Viceroy, mindful of the reaction against the deportation of the Punjabi leader Lala Lajpat Rai, refused to countenance any such move.

The court was presided over by Judge Leonard Birley. The prosecution was headed by Eardley Norton, a well-known advocate from Madras, hired by the Bengal government for the job. Aurobindo sat silently through the proceedings. He tried to distance himself from the courtroom and centre himself upon the unfolding universe within him:

At first, I tried to continue the inner life while sitting in the courtroom, but the unaccustomed mind would be attracted to every sound and sight, and the attempt would not succeed, in the midst of the noise going on all around. Later that feeling changed and I acquired the power to reject from the mind the immediate sounds and sights, and draw the mind inwards. But this did not take place in the early stages, the true power of concentration had not developed then. For that reason, giving up the futile attempt, I would be content with seeing, now and then, God in all creatures, for the rest I would observe the words and behaviour of my companions in adversity...[121]

The co-accused, the 'companions in adversity', many of whom had never seen him before, treated him with respect and reverence. The proceedings of the court, focused on such serious matters, should have been taking place in a serious and sober manner and atmosphere. Instead, it had the air of a country fair—there

---

[120]Ibid.
[121]Sri Aurobindo, *Tales of Prison Life*, Sri Aurobindo Ashram, 1974.

was laughter, heckling, jokes, cajoling—and the learned judge was constrained to issue the threat that he would have them chained, or stop their meals. Nothing worked. They carried on as before. Finally, they began to spend their time chatting and reading books, wholesome activities that Birley threatened to stop but, still, to no avail.

The proceedings stopped for a week in mid-June. When the court reconvened, Norton announced that one of the accused, Naren Goswami, had turned approver and would spill the beans on everybody. However, the judge refused to let the defence cross-examine Goswami. Listening to Goswami's testimony, Barin decided that it was time for them to make a break from prison. He hatched a plan and had weapons smuggled into prison. He decided that it was necessary that Aurobindo be informed of the proposed action. Aurobindo heard him out quietly, and finally said that he would rather wait for the trial to end. And that was that, as far as escape was concerned.

But Goswami's testimony, it was clear, could be the straw that broke the camel's back and lead to the undertrials being convicted. In order to save everybody from heavy punishment, it was imperative that Goswami be eliminated. Goswami was lured from his safe refuge in the European Quarter of the jail and killed by Satyen Bose and Kanailal Dutt on 31 August. They were both tried for the murder and given the death sentence.

Earlier, on 19 August, Aurobindo and 30 others were bound over for trial on charges of waging war against the king, which could lead to a death sentence. When the presiding judge appeared, Aurobindo immediately recognized him—it was his old Cambridge acquaintance, Charles Beachcroft.

The proceedings were similar to that of the preliminary trial, with two big differences. One was that the prosecution put forward two sets of documents as evidence to tie Aurobindo into Barin's group. The first documents were Aurobindo's letters to Mrinalini in which he spoke of his three madnesses. These really proved only his intense devotion to his country. The second, however, was potentially damaging. During the search at the time of Aurobindo's arrest, the police had seized what was apparently a letter written by Barin to his brother. In the letter, Barin spoke of sweets, which was interpreted as a reference to explosives.

The other crucial difference was that Aurobindo was represented by a new lawyer, the brilliant Chittaranjan Das. He forestalled Norton at every opportunity and won a critical victory when Beachcroft threw out Goswami's evidence because the defence had been denied a chance to examine him. After this, the case against Aurobindo was in tatters. Chittaranjan took head on the accusations against Aurobindo's writings: 'The doctrines he preaches are not doctrines of violence but doctrines of passive resistance... He says, believe in yourself; no one attains salvation who does not believe in himself. Similarly, he says, in the case of a nation.'[122]

Chittaranjan then rose to the heights of eloquence with a peroration that resonates through time:

> Long after this controversy is hushed in silence, long after this turmoil, this agitation ceases, long after he is dead and gone, he will be looked upon as the poet of patriotism, as the prophet of nationalism and the lover of humanity. Long after he is dead and gone, his words will be echoed and re-echoed not only in India, but across distant seas and lands. Therefore I say that the man in his position is not only standing before the bar of this Court but before the bar of the High Court of History.[123]

---

[122]Banerjee, Anurag (ed.), *Sri Aurobindo: His Political Life and Activities*, Overman Foundation, 2012.
[123]Ibid.

The verdict was delivered on 5 May 1909. Barin and Ullaskar were to be hanged (later commuted to life imprisonment on appeal), others were given sentences of varying length. Beachcroft spent 50 pages of the judgement on Aurobindo. He noted that if it had not been for the presence of Aurobindo, the case would have been over long ago. Beachcroft decided that the evidence against Aurobindo was too weak, given the gravity of the charges against him. Aurobindo was once again a free man.

7

The Karmayogin's Quiet Exit (1909–10)

The world that Aurobindo stepped out into on 6 May 1909 was very different from the one he had left on 5 May 1908. The dull, sullen silence that had been shattered by the cries of 'Bande Mataram' was back again. The people who had shown bravery had fallen behind again. But the Aurobindo who returned, too, was different from the Aurobindo who had gone into Alipore Jail. The spiritual side of his personality was becoming more and more strong, threatening to eclipse the political.

The Political Situation

The political landscape was bleak. Tilak had been exiled to Burma for six years. Lala Lajpat Rai and Bipin Chandra Pal had gone into voluntary exile to avoid Tilak's fate. Most of the Extremist leaders, including Subodh Mallick, had been jailed. In his 1948 note, Sri Aurobindo surveyed the political scenario:

> When he came out from jail, Sri Aurobindo found the whole political aspect of the country altered; most of the Nationalist leaders were in jail or in self-imposed exile and there was a general discouragement and depression, though the feeling in the country had not ceased but was only suppressed and

was growing by its suppression. He determined to continue the struggle; he held weekly meetings in Calcutta, but the attendance which had numbered formerly thousands full of enthusiasm was now only of hundreds and had no longer the same force and life.[124]

Aurobindo briefly flirted with the idea of a Home Rule movement of the kind that appeared just before the First World War or a passive resistance movement on the lines of what Mahatma Gandhi later carried out, but he resiled since he saw that 'he himself could not be the leader of such a movement.'[125] A harder self-appraisal by a politician cannot be imagined.

The hardliners were off the political battlefield, where the Moderates held sway. So much so that Gokhale could publicly proclaim, without fear of rebuttal, that it was madness to imagine that India could ever survive without British rule in the country. But the rebuttal that Gokhale did not expect, came from Aurobindo, who pointed out that while it may be madness, it had a method in it.

During this period, Aurobindo had to be cautious about what he said and did. The government kept him under constant surveillance. Bureaucratic circles were extremely unhappy at the turn of events, which saw Aurobindo, the biggest thorn in its side, set free. The results of the trials were examined by legal experts, and it was felt that while the government had substantive grounds on which to appeal the verdicts, there was no certainty of success. Reluctantly, it was decided that it would be necessary to wait till Aurobindo took a wrong step, before they could get ride of the pesky fellow. The death sentence having been lost, they hoped for the next best thing—deportation.

---

[124]*Complete Works of Sri Aurobindo: Volume 36: Autobiographical Notes and Other Writings of Historical Interest*, Sri Aurobindo Ashram, 1997, p. 47.
[125]Ibid.

Record of Yoga

After his release, Aurobindo received many invitations by numerous organizations to address public gatherings. He was, after all, the only Extremist leader still free. He decided to accept as many of these invitations, as they also offered an opportunity to study the situation on the ground and the thinking of the people. While travelling to Barisal by train and steamer for such an event, in his pocket diary—dated 17 June 1909—he made a few notes on the spiritual experiences that he was undergoing at the precise moment that they were taking place. Aurobindo continued, on and off, to record these experiences until 1927. These notes were finally published in 2001 as *Record of Yoga*, a title he used at several places in these notes. The two published volumes total over a thousand pages.

The record is very difficult to decipher and requires an understanding of the Sanskrit language and Hindu terminology. The importance and uniqueness of the record lies in the fact that, in a manner of speaking, it verifies for us Aurobindo's spiritual and philosophical thought. It verifies it in the sense that it makes clear that Aurobindo's philosophy is experiential rather than simply an intellectual, abstract or mental construct. At the same time, it is important to note that when Aurobindo expounded his philosophy, he did not refer to his own experiences but universalized it. The record has only a few entries scattered here and there that refer to his outer life. In a biographical sense, the book is important in making us understand that for Aurobindo, life was something that was being lived at several levels. While outwardly calm and sedate, and living an extremely busy and productive life, he was, psychologically and spiritually, living an incredibly intense internal life. One which was to continue till his death.

The Karmayogin

The *Bande Mataram* weekly had been shut down while Aurobindo was in jail. There was in Bengal, at that moment, no publication that could be used as an outlet for the propaganda of the Extremist movement. Aurobindo decided to start two publications to remedy the situation. The *Karmayogin* was published in English and the *Dharma* in Bengali. There was, however, a difference between Aurobindo's earlier writngs and now—while they were as fiery as ever and came close to breaking British laws, there was less emphasis on politics than in the earlier publications.

The principal contributor in *Karmayogin* and *Dharma* was, of course, Aurobindo himself. Launched on 19 June 1909, the *Karmayogin* proposed to be 'a weekly Review of National Religion, Literature, Science, Philosophy, etc.' Aurobindo wrote:

> We aim not at the alteration of a form of government but at the building up of a nation, Of that task, politics is a part, but only a part... we believe that that it is to make the ideal of human life that India rises today. It is a spiritual revolution we foresee and the material is only its shadow and reflex.[126]

He called upon the youth to recover India's lost spiritual past:

> Materially you are nothing, spiritually you are everything... First therefore become Indians. Recover the patrimony of your forefathers. Recover the Aryan thought, the Aryan discipline, the Aryan character, the Aryan life. Recover the Vedanta, the Gita, the yoga. Recover them not only in intellect or sentiment but in your lives... You must win back the kingdom of yourselves, the inner Swaraj, before you can win back your outer empire.[127]

---

[126]*Complete Works of Sri Aurobindo: Volume 8: Karmayogin,* Sri Aurobindo Ashram, 1997, p. 24.
[127]Ibid. 27.

In a startling passage that makes Aurobindo very much our contemporary, he wrote:

> We say to humanity, 'The time has come when you must take the great step and rise out of a material existence into the higher, deeper and wider life towards which humanity moves. The problems which have troubled mankind can only be solved by conquering the kingdom within, not by harnessing the forces of Nature to the service of comfort and luxury, but by mastering the forces of the intellect and the spirit.[128]

Unlike its legendary predecessor *Bande Mataram*, the *Karmayogin* was an instant hit and financially successful. Its success was so widespread that shortly afterwards, editions came out in Bengali, Hindi and Tamil. On 23 August, *Dharma*, the Bengali weekly edited by Aurobindo, too, came out. Aurobindo's command of Bengali had become stronger, though it was somewhat Sanskritized. He developed a unique style in Bengali, thanks to which it is possible to identify what he wrote.

The Uttarpara Speech

Among the many invitations that Aurobindo received, one came from a cultural organization in Uttarpara. The speech that he gave was unique, in that it was for the first time that he spoke of the spiritual crisis that he confronted in Alipore Jail. The Uttarpara speech, as it has come to be known, has also, like his Bombay oration, acquired notoriety for its supposed communal bias.

Aurobindo rose to speak on 30 May 1909 at Uttarpara. The opening sentences made it clear to the listeners that they were about to hear one of the most momentous speeches in modern Indian history: 'As I sat here, there came into my mind a word

---

[128]Ibid. 19.

that I have to speak to you, a word that I have to speak to the whole of the Indian Nation. It was spoken first to myself in jail and I have come out of jail to speak it to my people...'[129]

After a completely open description of what he had undergone in jail and its results, he concluded that Sanatana Dharma is nationalism. It is this equation of Sanatana Dharma with nationalism that has proved to be problematic to many, as it supposedly displays a bias towards Hinduism. This completely ignores what Aurobindo said about Hinduism in the speech itself—that it could not be bound by a single country and belongs to the world. Moreover, in the essay 'The Ideal of the Karmayogin', published in the same issue in which the speech was printed, Aurobindo gave a definition of Sanatana Dharma in the widest sense of the term: 'The religion which embraces Science and faith, Theism, Christianity, Mahomedanism and Buddhism and yet is none of these, is that to which the World-Spirit moves.' He added, 'This Sanatana Dharma has many scriptures, Veda, Vedanta, Gita, Upanishad, Darshana, Puranas, Tantra, nor could it reject the Bible or the Koran; but its real, most authoritative scripture is in the heart in which the Eternal has His dwelling.'[130]

The Hooghly Conference

The Bengal Congress, still precariously united, met at Hooghly, where, of course, the Moderates had support. Before the conference took place, a meeting of the Extremists also took place, where the young hotheads discussed how to break up the conference, if their demands were not met. Aurobindo responded:

> Do you have any idea what great work Surendranath Banerjea and his Moderate Party have done in Bengal politics? I shall

---

[129]Ibid. 3.
[130]Ibid. 26.

not be a party to bringing down their downfall by foul means. We shall fully respect the Moderate Party and place before the conference, in clear terms, our stand of independence. If our ideal is sacred and lofty and just, the Conference cannot but give its verdict in our favour. If you do not accept this policy, I shall withdraw from this Conference.[131]

After this remarkable display behind closed doors, Aurobindo did exactly the same thing in public. When their resolution was blocked, the Extremists created a ruckus. Aurobindo stood up and raised his hand, and the noise immediately subsided. Aurobindo announced that the Extremists, though they appeared to be in a majority, would withdraw for the sake of party unity. And that is exactly what happened. The Extremists withdrew, and the Moderate resolution was passed. Aurobindo, who had not hesitated to break the Congress at Surat, equally did not hesitate to preserve its unity at the Hooghly conference.

At about this time, word came from different sources, including Sister Nivedita, to Aurobindo that the government was planning to attack the nationalists again, and this time they would use the weapon of deportation. Aurobindo decided to pre-empt any such move. He wrote in the *Karmayogin* on 31 July 1909: 'Rumour is strong that a case for my deportation has been submitted to the Government by the Calcutta Police and neither the Tranquility of the country nor the scrupulous legality of our procedure is a guarantee against the contingency of the all-powerful fiat of the Government watchdogs silencing scruples on the part of those who advise at Simla.'[132] He speculated that perhaps the action may not take place because of possible scruples in England, and his status as Public Enemy No. 1 for the regime. He appeared to

---

[131]Athalaya, V.V., 'My Life-Story', *Mother India*, January 1972.
[132]*Complete Works of Sri Aurobindo: Volume 8: Karmayogin,* Sri Aurobindo Ashram, 1997, p. 150.

have staved off the danger for the time being.

But then, one day in February 1910, a young man came agitatedly to the office and said that an arrest warrant had been issued in the name of Aurobindo. While the others talked animatedly, Aurobindo sat quietly. Then, he suddenly stood up and announced that they were leaving. Later, he said that an inner voice he knew well had told him to go to Chandernagore, a nearby French enclave. They then proceeded to the banks of the river Hooghly, where they hired a boat and left for Chandernagore.

Chandernagore: First Refuge

When they reached Chandernagore the next morning, they approached Charuchandra Roy, a former freedom fighter, who was a fellow inmate during Aurobondo's time at the Alipore Jail. Scarred by his experience, and afraid of the eminence and notoriety of his new would-be guest, he refused them shelter. After they left, ashamed of his cowardice, he informed another friend of his, Motilal Roy, about the arrival of Aurobindo. Motilal immediately ran towards the river, saw the boat and hailed them. He asked if Aurobindo was on the boat, and after Aurobindo's identity was confirmed, Motilal led the refugees to his nearby house.

Aurobindo hid in a small room in Motilal's house, with the household learning of his presence by chance. As a precaution, from time to time, he was shifted to other places. He spent his time in meditating and writing. However, rumours of his disappearance from Calcutta and presence in Chandernagore began to circulate. Chandernagore, being a small town, was also not safe from the point of security. British agents could easily have kidnapped him from there.

Meanwhile, back in Calcutta, rumours flew fast and furious about Aurobindo's whereabouts, with his absence having been noted. Sister Nivedita, at the request of Aurobindo, had taken charge of the running of *Karmayogin*, and for some time, a few articles Aurobindo had written and left behind were published, while the rest did not come out in his lifetime. A light piece mocking the rumours was published on 19 March 1910: 'We are greatly astonished to learn from the local Press that Sj. Aurobindo Ghose has disappeared from Calcutta and the fact is unknown to his other Koshas. Only as he requires perfect solitude and freedom from disturbance for some his Sadhan for some time, his address is being kept a strict secret...'[133]

Into Exile

But with everybody—and especially the British—searching for Aurobindo, it was clear that Chandernagore was no longer safe. Around this time, Aurobindo received yet another adesh. This time, he was told to go to Pondicherry, a French enclave in South India, near Madras. Aurobindo sent Suresh, one of his assistants, to Pondicherry to find a refuge for him there.

Aurobindo made it to back to Calcutta unscathed. Using a false name, he boarded the ship *SS Dupleix*, accompanied by Bijoy Nag, and left Calcutta in the darkness. They reached Pondicherry on 4 April 1910 at four in the afternoon. Aurobindo never left Pondicherry again. Incredibly, his active political life lasted only three and a half years—of which a full year was spent in jail.

The Karmayogin's Last Words...

Meanwhile, the last of Aurobindo's writing to appear in the *Karmayogin* was in the issue dated 26 March 1910, titled 'In Either Case'. In this essay, he foreshadows his future: 'The work that was begun at Dakshineshwar is far from finished, it is not

---

[133]Ibid. 461.

even understood. That which Vivekananda received and strove to develop, has not yet materialized.' And on the future of the world, he wrote: 'A less discreet revelation prepares, a more concrete force manifests, but where it comes, when it comes, none knoweth.'[134]

Shortly afterwards, the *Karmayogin*, helmed briefly by Sister Nivedita, quietly closed shop. But before his departure, Aurobindo the Karmayogin left a warning to his countrymen, which has stood the test of time: 'The winning of freedom is an easy task, the keeping of it is less easy. The first needs only one tremendous effort in which all the energies of the country must be concentrated, the second requires united, organized and settled strength.'[135]

---

[134]Ibid. 462.
[135]Ibid. 464.

8

The Religion of Nationalism

Aurobindo's ideas—poliitical, social and cultural—continued to develop, evolve and mature during the Calcutta years, with his writings appearing in *Bande Mataram* and *Karmayogin*, *Yugantar* and *Dharma*. Most of Aurobindo's articles addressed the issue of the day, and thus, at that time, he had built no systematic political theory—if anybody had asked him, he would probably have said that it all boiled down to swaraj through passive resistance and boycott. However, he did systematically put down his ideas on passive resistance—possibly the first time it was so named in India—in a series of essays published in *Bande Mataram*.

Swaraj

Swaraj lay at the heart of the demands of the Extremists. It was a word that meant different things to different people. The word could be translated as self-rule, but that, too, depended who was using the word. In the case of the Moderates, it meant colonial self-government as a part of the British Empire. For the Extremists, the word meant total independence from Britain. Or in Aurobindo's close-to-the-edge style of writing: 'Swaraj is the only goal which the heart of Bengal recognizes, Swaraj without limitations or reservation.' He also said:

Swaraj emphasizes the idea of self-sufficiency and insists on it. It mitigates against the idea of there being any limit to our expansion. We must be full, we must be perfect, we are the divinity in embryo and when fully developed we shall be co-extensive with God Himself. That is what Swaraj unmistakably means. It at once embodies the idea of independence, unity, liberty.[136]

Aurobindo asserted:

Boycott is good, not for the good of boycott but for the good of Swaraj. Swadeshi is good, not for the good of Swadeshi, not for the good of Swaraj but for the sake of Swaraj. Arbitration is good, not for the sake of arbitration but for the sake of Swaraj. If we forget Swaraj and win anything else we shall be like the seeker whose belt was turned indeed to gold but the stone of alchemy was lost for ever.[137]

He pointed out that progress had been made by the nationalists only because of the promise they had made that their aim was swaraj. Not only that, they were determined to get it not through requesting it as a gift from the British but by asserting their alienable right for it. A docile people could never get swaraj, but a people who were ready to fight for it could.

For Aurobindo, swaraj was not just political, it was spiritual too; the two were linked together. Political swaraj was an empty vessel if it focused only on the material world. For it to be complete, spiritual freedom, too, was necessary. And spiritual freedom, too, needed the political act of freedom, in order to be itself complete. He pointed out, 'spiritual freedom can never be the lot of many in a land of slaves. A few may follow the path of the Yogin and

---

[136]*Complete Works of Sri Aurobindo: Volume 6: Bande Mataram—I–II*, Sri Aurobindo Ashram, 1997, p. 263.
[137]Ibid.

rise above their surroundings, but the mass of men cannot ever take the first step towards spiritual salvation... By our political freedom we shall once more recover our spiritual freedom.'

Aurobindo emphasized that swaraj as defined by the Extremists was their ultimate goal. They were not ready for any half-measures, such as reformed councils or simply ICS examinations or more Indians in the ICS, etc. They had a clear-cut goal, and they honed their methods towards achieving it. And that method was passive resistance.

Passive Resistance

Aurobindo published a seven-part series on passive resistence in the *Bande Mataram* in April 1907. He began with the premise that the self-development of a nation can be done by that nation alone. It cannot be done in a land of slaves. It was, therefore, necessary to achieve freedom before any attempt could be made to uplift the country. And that was possible only if, first, there was a central, directing organization: 'Industrially, socially, educationally there can be no genuine progress carrying the whole nation forward, unless there is a central force representing either the best thought and energy of the country or else the majority of its citizens and able to enforce the views and decisions of the nation on all its constituent members.'[138] But this alone was not enough. Aurobindo emphasized that 'we have therefore not only to organize a central authority, not only to take up all branches of our national life into our hands, but in order to meet bureaucratic opposition and to compel the alien control to remove its hold on us, if not at once, then tentacle by tentacle we must organize defensive resistance.'[139]

---

[138]Ibid. 265.
[139]Ibid. 266.

But this resistance must have an aim. It must not simply be resistance for the sake of resistance—it must have a focused goal, which is sought to be achieved. He pointed out that though the agitation in Bengal was precipitated by one event—the partition of the province—its aim went beyond this narrow objective. Aurobindo wrote:

> At a bound we passed therefore, from mere particular grievances, however serious and intolerable, to the use of passive resistance as a means of cure for the basest and evilest feature of the present system—the bleeding to death of a country by foreign exploitation. And from that we are steadily advancing...to the one true objective of all resistance—the creation of a free popular Government and the vindication of Indian liberty.[140]

But if there is to be resistance, and it must have an objective, it is imperative to be certain of its necessity. What is the necessity of passive resistance in the particular Indian context? Aurobindo's answer: 'The advocates of self-development and defensive resistance are no extremists but are trying to give the country its last chance of escaping the necessity of extremism.'[141] Here, Aurobindo warned that if passive resistance was not resorted to, something much worse could take its place.

And what are the methods of passive resistance? According to Aurobindo:

> The first principle of passive resistance, therefore, which the new school have placed in the forefront of their programme, is to make administration under pressure conditions impossible by an organised refusal to do anything which shall help either British commerce in the exploitation of the

---

[140]Ibid.
[141]Ibid. 280.

country or British officialdom in the administration of it, unless and until the conditions are changed in the manner and to the extent demanded by the people. This attitude is summed up in the one word, Boycott.[142]

Passive resistance also places certain obligations upon the passive resister. This is to break an illegal law, if it so becomes necessary. Aurobindo insisted, 'the new spirit will not suffer any individual aspiring to speak or act on behalf of the people to palter with the obligations of high truthfulness and unflinching courage without which no one has a claim to lead or instruct his fellow-countrymen.'[143]

But passive resistance, too, has its limits. Much pressure is brought upon the passive resister, and sometimes it becomes very difficult to withstand it. It is, therefore, incumbent upon the resister to assess whether it is being effective or not. If the answer is in the negative, then it must be discarded. 'If the bureaucracy were to become so oppressive as to render a struggle for liberty on the lines we have indicated, impossible; if after a fair trial given to this method, the object with which we undertook it, proved to be as far off as ever...'[144] then it should be discarded.

The passive resistance series is an exquisitely written work. It is well and closely argued, and is extraordinary in its ability to balance extremes, find a fine line to walk the talk and yet sound firm and logical in its intent. It exemplifies the best of Aurobindo's thinking at that point of time in his life. It is unquestionably a precursor of sorts to the writings of the future Mahatma on satyagraha.

---

[142]Ibid.
[143]Ibid. 289.
[144]Ibid.

The Communal Tag

Let us take a look at a persistent charge against Sri Aurobindo, then and even now, that there is an anti-Muslim bias in his writings, which reflected his pro-Hindu stance. We shall answer this question by examining his writings of the time itself, specifically concerning the Muslims, and his criticism of his friend Lala Lajpat Rai.

We have already seen Aurobindo's sharp comments at the time of the 1907 riots, where, having called out the Muslims as the perpetrators of the attacks on Hindus, he refused to call the Hindus victims or to stigmatize the Muslims, and instead pointed at the British as the instigators of the riots. Aurobindo did not want to exclude Muslims from his vision of a new Indian nation but to integrate them into it. He wrote:

> We do not shun, we desire the awakening of Islam in India even if its first crude efforts are misdirected against ourselves... Of one thing we may be certain, that Hindu-Mahomedan unity cannot be effected by political adjustments or Congress flatteries. It must be sought deeper down, in the heart and the mind, for where the causes of disunion are, there the remedies must be sought.[145]

Aurobindo called for an emotional integration of Hindu–Muslim identities, and, at the same time, to rise above them for a common Indian identity. Idealistic, such a recommendation certainly was, but nevertheless, it stands true. If the solution that he offered seemed to be rather simple, it must be noted that none of those who followed Aurobindo in the years to come as leaders of the nationalist movement, had anything better to offer.

When the British came up with the idea of separate electorates for Muslims, in order to ensure that they were not 'oppressed'

---

[145]Ibid. 259.

by the Hindu majority, and if indeed the intent of the scheme had actually been minority protection, then it should have been extended to the Sikhs, Parsis and Christians. Aurobindo emphasized that:

> We will not for a moment accept separate electorates or separate representation, not because we are opposed to a large Mahomedan influence in popular assemblies when they come, but because we will be no party to a distinction which recognizes Hindu and Mahomedan as permanently separate political units and thus precludes the growth of a single and indivisible Indian nation.[146]

Aurobindo's most sustained and trenchant observations on the Hindu–Muslim question appeared in the *Karmayogin* in 1909. It discussed the rise of the Muslim League but especially the establishment of the Hindu Sabha by Lala Lajpat Rai, Aurobindo's friend and comrade. Aurobindo wrote:

> Lala Lajpat Rai struck a higher note, that of Hindu nationalism as a necessary preliminary to a greater Indian Nationality. We distrust this ideal... we do not understand Hindu nationalism as a possibility under modern conditions. Hindu nationalism had a meaning in the time of Shivaji and Ramdas, when the object of national revival was to overthrow a Mahomedan domination which, once tending to Indian unity and toleration, had become oppressive and disruptive.[147]

What was Aurobindo's vision of a future India in this respect? He proclaimed that 'Our ideal therefore is an Indian nationality,

---

[146]*Complete Works of Sri Aurobindo: Volume 8: Karmayogin*, Sri Aurobindo Ashram, 1997, p. 289.
[147]Ibid. 303.

largely Hindu in spirit...but wide enough also to include the Moslem and his culture and traditions and absorb them into itself.' This is the same as the common nationality sought by all leaders of the nationalist movement, including Gandhi and Nehru. It is obvious that it is a travesty of the truth to describe Aurobindo as a Hindu communalist.

Here, it is necessary to take a break from chronology and go to an interesting exchange of correspondence between Sri Aurobindo and a Muslim visitor to his ashram, as they touch on the communal question. In 1932, the visitor, who we shall call X, wrote to Sri Aurobindo, 'Had Mahomedanism no message for India? Is this a teaching of the Ashram?' Sri Aurobindo answered, 'No, certainly not; it is a sheer misinterpretation of my views. I have written clearly that the coming of so many religions to India was a part of her destiny and a great advantage for the work to be done.'[148] When asked why Muslims have been excluded from his yoga, he shot back a long explanation:

> It is news to me that I have excluded Mahomedans from the Yoga. I have not done it any more than I have excluded Europeans or Christians. As for giving up one's past, if that means giving up the outer forms of the old religions, it is done as much by the Hindus here as by the Mahomedans. Every Hindu here—even those who were orthodox Brahmins and have grown old in it, give up all observance of caste, take food from Pariahs and are served by them, associate and eat with Mahomedans, Christians, Europeans, cease to practice temple worship or Sandhya (daily prayers) and mantras, accept a non-Hindu from Europe as their spiritual director. What is kept of Hinduism is Vedanta and Yoga, in which Hinduism is one with Sufism of Islam and with

---

[148]*Complete Works of Sri Aurobindo: Volume 35: Letters on Himself and the Ashram,* Sri Aurobindo Ashram, 1997, p. 700.

the Christian mystics... If I have used Sanskrit terms and figures, it is because I know them and do not know Persian and Arabic. I have not the slightest objection to anyone here drawing inspiration from Islamic sources...

Aurobindo's nationalism, while predicated on an evocation of Hindu values, was in no way directed against other religions. It was in no way discriminatory and exclusionary. It was, as we have seen, inclusive to a staggering degree, as is made clear when one considers his wide interpretation of Sanatana Dharma. It is an understanding of what is meant by nationalism that India can benefit from even today.

Section III

The Lover of Humanity

9

The Arya, The Mother, the Ashram (1910–47)

The Nagaswamis were a large group of ascetics who lived near Pondicherry. When their leader, Nagai Japta, was about to die, he said that a great yogi from the north would come 30 years later. He would practise a poorna yoga—Integral Yoga—and there would be three signs to indicate that he was the expected one. Sri Aurobindo, of course, practised Integral Yoga. The three madnesses described in his letter to Mrinalini could be considered to be the three signs. When Sri Aurobindo reached Pondicherry, many who knew of the prophecy thought it had been fulfilled.

Pondicherry: The Last Refuge

At the time, Pondicherry was a quiet, laidback and sleepy coastal colony of the French. It was also a place where many people who were not in the good books of the British would take refuge, so Sri Aurobindo had good company. Sri Aurobindo, on arrival, went to stay at the house of a wealthy businessman supporter, Sankara Chettiar. All the arrangements had been made by Suresh, who had contacted a supporter of the nationalists, Srinivasachariar. Suresh had given him a letter written by Sri Aurobindo.

At first suspicious, as in Pondicherry the nationalists were shadowed by both the French Police and spies sent by the British, Srinivasachariar had accepted that the letter was genuine and made arrangements for stay at Chettiar's house, where the entire second floor was given over to the new arrivals. Plans for a grand reception were shelved when Suresh urgently insisted that Sri Aurobindo did not want any publicity and that his arrival should be kept a secret. Pondicherry being a small town, rumours about his arrival had already spread with lightning speed.

Sri Aurobindo led a secluded life for the next three months. At one point, he decided to fast for 23 days. The only visitors he had were Bharathi, a young, fiery Tamil nationalist poet, with whom Sri Aurobindo had many conversations, and Rangaswamy Iyengar, a descendant of the Nagaswami's disciple. Hearing about Sri Aurobindo's arrival, he had become convinced that this was the long-expected Uttara Yogi (yogi from the north).

Sri Aurobindo spent many hours in meditation and tried his hand at automatic writing. The result was published by Iyengar as *Yogic Sadhan*, which specifically mentioned edited by the Uttara Yogi. Sri Aurobindo took great pains, over the years, to point out that it was not really written by him, and therefore, should not be taken as a commentary upon his own system of yoga.

Back in Calcutta, the long-awaited police raid took place, and a number of documents were taken away from the offices of the *Karmayogin*. There was an arrest warrant out for Sri Aurbindo and a case filed against him for sedition. Yet again, while the printer was sentenced to prison, Sri Aurobindo got off scot-free. If he wished, he could return to Calcutta. Sri Aurobindo did not, and he made it clear soon after that he was no longer politically active and was now fully engaged in his yoga. He wrote a letter to *The Hindu* in November 1910, explaining that he was in Pondicherry and had left the political field:

I left British India over a month before proceedings were taken against me and, as I had purposely retired here in order to pursue my Yogic Sadhna undisturbed by political action or pursuit and had already severed connection with my political work, I did not feel called upon to surrender on the warrant for sedition, as might have been incumbent on me if I had remained in the political field.[149]

He wrote that his place of stay was known to the British, and he would not engage in political correspondence and would instead await the verdict. Ironically, the verdict was published in the same issue as his letter.

Meeting Paul Richard

One day, Sri Aurobindo was informed that a gentleman from Paris wanted to meet him. Paul Richard had come to Pondicherry to contest the seat for French India in the elections to the French parliament. However, he was replaced by another person. Richard decided to stay on, as he was spiritually curious. A former military man, he had studied for the clergy and also the law. He was married to Mirra Alfassa, with whom he pursued his spiritual quest. He asked to meet a yogi, and they spoke of Sri Aurobindo. He did not want to meet Richard, as he thought that he was probably just another spiritual tourist.

However, Sri Aurobindo was prevailed upon to meet Richard, as Srinivasachariar and Bharathi thought his political connections might come in use if there was any problem with the French authorities. Sri Aurobindo and Richard hit it off when they finally met. Richard asked the meaning of the Star of David, with ascending and descending triangles, and a lotus at the centre.

---

[149]*Complete Works of Sri Aurobindo: Volume 36: Autobiographical Notes and Other Writings of Historical Interest*, Sri Aurobindo Ashram, 1997, p. 264

Sri Aurobindo told him that it symbolized the opening of the consciousness to the Divine. Sri Aurobindo would later adopt it as his own symbol. Richard, afterwards, always spoke highly of Sri Aurobindo, even after differences arose between them. This meeting was another major turning point in Sri Aurobindo's life, as it initiated contact with Mirra, who joined Richard in corresponding with Sri Aurobindo.

Life in Pondicherry

The spartan lifestyle that Sri Aurobindo had been forced to lead since childhood, which had become second nature to him, continued. It had helped to sustain him in jail and came to his aid now. The small band had left Chettiar's house and moved from place to place until 1913, when they settled at Rue Francois Martin. The small band, their meager numbers augmented by Nolini Kanta Gupta, who had found his way there after being found not guilty in the Alipore case, lived in privation and were constantly on the alert for Sri Aurobindo's safety. Nolini would become a much-respected mainstay of the ashram till his death in the 1980s.

There was fear that the British, who had their agents in Pondicherry, might attempt to kidnap Sri Aurobindo. One man was always on alert, and bottles of acid were kept at hand to stop any such attempt. These fears were reinforced by the failed attempt of a British agent to suggest that the revolutionaries were planning a terrorist attack in Pondicherry itself. Some forged documents were put in an earthen pot and buried in the garden of the house of V.V.S. Aiyar, a Tamil revolutionary who had fled Madras. The pot was found by Aiyar's servant. Aiyar immediately showed it to Sri Aurobindo. Sri Aurobindo told him to show it to the French authorities, which Aiyar did. As result, Sri Aurobindo's residence was also searched. The French magistrate, astonished by the Greek, Latin and works in other languages present there, exclaimed that this was a scholar, not a terrorist, and stopped the search. After this, the group relaxed their guard a bit. Over the years, the French authorities stopped looking at Sri Aurobindo as a security risk, and the British also gave up their attempts to get their hands on him, realizing that he had well and truly left politics behind. They never again made the mistake of going after him, to end up with egg on their faces. A message was also conveyed to Sri Aurobindo that he could return to British India without any fear of arrest, an offer he studiously ignored.

The small group lead a very simple life, eating meals consisting of lentils and rice. They passed their time in studies. Sri Aurobindo once again took up his job as a teacher, but this time that of a private tutor—he taught his motley crew Greek, Latin and French! He also introduced them to the delights of world literature, such as Dante in Italian. He was constantly practising yoga and meditating, and he would candidly impart to his companious his new-found understanding and guide them in their own experiments, which was to become his lifelong occupation.

Sri Aurobindo's address had become public, and he was constantly pestered by unwelcome visitors, who forced their presence upon him and became a nuisance, trying to peep in through doors and windows. Exasperated, he again wrote a letter to *The Hindu*, saying that he does not receive visitors, as they disturb his sadhana. Futhermore, all accounts of meetings with him were fanciful. The only visitor Sri Aurobindo saw at the time was the French adventurer and explorer Alexandra David-Néel.

The biggest problem that Sri Aurobindo had at this time was that of finances. Sri Aurobindo and his followers received a small sum from K.V.R. Iyengar, but it did not go far. None of them were earning money from a job. Sri Aurobindo depended upon small donations from here and there, which helped to make ends meet. He also appealed to Motilal Roy to help collect money. Sri Aurobindo humourously spoke of this trying time: 'No doubt, God will provide, but He has contracted a peculiar habit of waiting till the last moment. I only hope He does not wish us to learn how to live on a minute quantity like Bharathi.'[150]

Then, one day, just as 20 years ago in Baroda, Barin suddenly turned up in Pondicherry. Sentenced to life imprisonment after his death sentence was commuted, he had been sent to the penal colony in the Andamans. Freed at the end of the First World War, he had, once again, made his way to his older brother's house.

The Literary Life

During the early years in Pondicherry, Sri Aurobindo wrote a number of poems and plays, largely drawing upon his Greek studies. The most ambitious was *Ilion*, divided into nine books and totaling 5,000 lines. It drew upon Homer's Iliad and focused on the last day of Troy—Ilion is another name for Troy. Why Troy? Sri Aurobindo believed that the fall of Troy was one of the hinge moments in world history, and the event led to a new path opening up for humankind. He also wrote a number of plays— *Eric, Rodogune, The Viziers of Bassora, Perseus the Deliverer* and *Vasavadutta*. Sri Aurobindo also embarked on the writing of his great epic, *Savitri*.

Sri Aurobindo made a new departure in Pondicherry as far as linguistics was concerned. As we have seen, his interest in Sanskrit had arisen in England. In Baroda, he read the classic Sanskrit poems and plays. As far as religion or spirituality was concerned, he studied the Upanishads and also published some translations during the Calcutta years. However, while he had some acquaintance with the Vedas, it was only in Pondicherry

---

[150]Ibid. 175.

that he studied them seriously and systematically for the first time, leading to translations and commentaries.

Aurobindo's interest in linguistics was aroused by his study of Tamil, which he had begun to learn. During his time, and even today, it is generally assumed that the Dravidian families of language spoken in South India have no relationship whatsoever with Indo-European languages, which include Sanskrit. Sri Aurobindo believed that it was otherwise and presented a number of evidence backing this view. Sri Aurobindo, thus, offered a new interpretation of the origins of language, going against the grain of the prevailing academic thought.

Mirra

After David-Néel, the next visitors that Sri Aurobindo welcomed in Pondicherry were Paul Richard and his wife, Mirra. The couple arrived in 1914 and immediately met Sri Aurobindo in the afternoon of 29 March. When Mirra saw Sri Aurobindo, she recognized him immediately as the person she had seen in a few visions, as she noted: 'As soon as I saw Sri Aurobindo I recognised in him the well-known being whom I used to call Krishna.'[151] While talking, she told Sri Aurobindo that she had a problem trying to achieve complete silence. A few minutes later, what she wanted, took place. In her journal, Mirra wrote of her reaction to meeting Sri Aurobindo: 'It matters little that there are thousands of beings plunged in the densest ignorance. He whom we saw yesterday is on earth; his presence is enough to prove that a day will come when darkness shall be transformed into light, and Thy reign shall indeed be established upon earth.'[152]

---

[151]Iyengar, K.R. Srinivasa, *On the Mother: The Chronicle of a Manifestation and Ministry*, Sri Aurobindo International Centre of Education, 1994.
[152]*Collected Works of the Mother, Volume 1, Prayers & Meditations*, Sri Aurobindo Ashram, 2003, p. 113.

Blanche Rachel Mirra Alfassa was born in Paris on 21 February 1878 to Sephardic Jews who had come to France from Egypt. Mirra had had mystical experiences throughout her childhood and youth. At the age of 15, she joined the Académie Julian, an art institute. She married the painter Henri Morriset, and they had a son, Andre, in 1898. She moved in mystical circles and came in contact with Max Theon and his wife, who were occultists. Mirra's marriage with Morriset came to an end in 1908, and soon after, she met Paul Richard. Richard used to give impressive talks on mysticism. Mirra married Richard, though there was not much of a meeting of minds between them.

Richard had come to Pondicherry to yet again contest the election, and this time, he actually stood. However, he failed to connect with the voters and lost by a big margin. Instead of returning to Paris, it was decided that the trio would collaborate on a bilingual philosophical journal, to be called *Arya* in English and *Revue de la Grande Synthese* (Review of Grand Synthesis) in French. Its purpose was 'a systematic study of the highest problems of existence' and also 'the formation of a vast synthesis of knowledge, harmonizing the diverse religious traditions of humanity, occidental as well as oriental', and to aim at '...the unification of intellectual and scientific disciplines with those of intuitive experience.'[153]

The outbreak of the war in Europe forced Richard and Mirra to leave Pondicherry. Before his departure, Richard transferred all rights of the new journal to Sri Aurobindo. The 64-page journal would now be prepared by Sri Aurobindo alone. It was a fateful choice—all of Sri Aurobindo's major works—*The Life Divine*, *The Synthesis of Yoga*, *The Secret of the Veda*, *The Ideal of Human Unity* and *The Human Cycle*—as well as many Sanskrit translations,

---

[153]Iyengar, K.R. Srinivasa, *On the Mother: The Chronicle of a Manifestation and Ministry*, Sri Aurobindo International Centre of Education, 1994.

appeared in *Arya*. *The Future Poetry* and *The Foundations of Indian Culture*, in part, came from writings in *Arya*. Only *The Mother*, *Essays on the Gita* and *Savitri* did not first see the light of day in *Arya*.

The first issue was published on 15 August 1914 and the last in 1921, and was very successful, earning a surplus. It was discontinued because Sri Aurobindo simply did not have the time to focus on it. In the second issue, Sri Aurobindo explained why the journal was given the name 'Arya', in reply to a question posed by a reader. He rejected the racial and linguistic meanings attached to the term Arya, and gave his own particular understanding of the word: 'Intrinsically, in its most fundamental sense, Arya means an effort or an uprising and overcoming. The Aryan is he who strives and overcomes all outside him and within him that stands opposed to the human advance.' Sri Aurobindo continued, 'The word Arya expressed a particular ethical and social ideal, an ideal of well-governed life, candour, courtesy, nobility, straight dealing, courage, gentleness, purity, humanity, social duty, eagerness for knowledge, respect for the wise and learned, the social accomplishments.'[154]

The Last Interview

Sri Aurobindo, withdrawing further into a life of seclusion, gave a rare interview to *The Hindu*, on 4 January 1915, which also may have been the last that he ever gave. The answers that he gave are intriguing, in that they present a link to the past, and an intimation of the way his thinking was moving at this moment in time.

When asked his reaction to the 1914 Congress, Sri Aurobindo replied: 'I do not find the proceedings of the Christmas Conference

---

[154]*Complete Works of Sri Aurobindo: Volume 13: Essays in Philosophy and Yoga*, Sri Aurobindo Ashram, 1997, p. 441.

very interesting and inspiring. They seem to me mere repitions of the petty and lifeless formulas of the past and hardly show any sense of the great breadth of the future that is blowing upon us.'[155] He then spoke a line of thought that was to become increasingly familiar in the next few years: 'The old, petty forms and little narrow, make-believe activities are getting out of date. The world is changing rapidly around us and preparing for more colossal changes in the future. We must rise to the greatness of thought and action which it will demand upon the nations who hope to live.'

When asked what should be done in order for India to realize its destiny, he answered:

> Only by a general intellectual and spiritual awakening can this nation fulfil its destiny. Our limited information, our second-hand intellectual activities, our bounded interests, our narrow life of little family aims and small money-getting have prevented us from entering into the broad life of the world. Fortunately, there are ever-increasing signs of a widened outlook, a richer intellectual output and numerous sparks of liberal genius which show that the necessary change is coming No nation in modern times can grow great by politics alone. A rich and varied life, life, energetic in all its parts, is the condition of a sound, vigorous national existence. From this point of view, also the last few five years have been a great benefit to the country.'[156]

The Mother

After returning to Paris, Richard and Mirra left to spend four years in Japan. Richard had been found medically unfit for military

[155]'Sri Aurobindo at Pondicherry 8', auromaa.org, https://tinyurl.com/23wvn7m8. Accessed on 3 June 2022.
[156]Ibid.

service and found a job as a trade representative in Japan. They finally returned to Pondicherry in 1920. However, the relationship between Mirra and Richard came to an end when she realized that it was not possible to change his nature. Richard left, and Mirra stayed on with her companion Dorothy Hodgson. When a storm damaged the house she was living in, Sri Aurobindo invited her to move into his own house. She accepted and lived as his spiritual collaborator for the rest of his life.

One of the most important works of Sri Aurobindo is *The Mother*, a brief work partly written as letters to some disciples and published in 1928. It is Sri Aurobindo's most accessible writing and an excellent introduction to his spiritual philosophy, but is at times overlooked or minimized in studies of his life. He began with the magnificent line, 'There are two powers that alone can effect in their conjunction the great and difficult thing which is the aim of our endeavour, a fixed and unfailing aspiration that calls from below and a supreme grace from above that answers. The power that mediates between the sanction and the call is the presence and power of the Divine Mother.'[157] A sadhak or disciple will have to be an aspirant, ready to surrender oneself and reject negatives such as pride and arrogance. 'The more complete your sincerity, faith and surrender, the more will grace and protection be with you.'[158]

Sri Aurobindo then writes of the four aspects of The Mother in a remarkable passage of great power:

> Four aspects of the Mother, four of her leading Powers and Personalities have stood in front in her guidance of this universe and in her dealings with the terrestrial play. One is her personality of calm wideness and comprehending wisdom

---

[157]*Complete Works of Sri Aurobindo: Volume 32: The Mother with Letters on the Mother*, Sri Aurobindo Ashram, 1997, p. 3.
[158]Ibid. 8

and tranquil benignity and inexhaustible compassion and sovereign and surpassing majesty and all-ruling greatness. Another embodies her power of splendid strength and irresistible passion, her warrior mood, her overwhelming will, her impetuous swiftness and world-shaking force. A third is vivid and sweet and wonderful with her deep secret of beauty and harmony and fine rhythm, her intricate and subtle opulence, her compelling attraction and captivating grace. The fourth is equipped with her close and profound capacity of intimate knowledge and careful flawless work and quiet and exact perfection in all things. Wisdom, Strength, Harmony, Perfection are their several attributes and it is these powers that they bring with them into the world, manifest in a human disguise in their Vibhutis and shall found in the divine degree of their ascension in those who can open their earthly nature to the direct and living influence of the Mother. To the four we give the four great names, Maheshwari, Mahakali, Mahalakshmi, Mahasaraswati.[159]

Mirra, over time, came to be known as The Mother, and was explicitly recognized by Sri Aurobindo as the embodiment of what he had written about in *The Mother*. On 24 November 1926, an extraordinary event took place. The 24 people sitting and talking to Sri Aurobindo felt a great power in the atmosphere. Sri Aurobindo explained in letters written in 1935 what had happened: 'The 24th November 1926 was the descent of Krishna into the physical. Krishna is not the supramental Light. The descent of Krishna would mean the descent of the Overmind Godhead preparing, though not itself actually, the descent of Supermind and Ananda. Krishna is the Anand-maya, he supports the evolution through

---

the Overmind leading it towards his Ananda.'[160]

Shotly afterwards, Sri Aurobindo told Barin to tell the others: 'Mirra is my Shakti. She has taken charge of the new creation. You will get everything from her. Give consent to whatever she wants to do.'[161] Sri Aurobindo handed over to The Mother the running of the community around him, which would become known as the Sri Aurobindo Ashram. Sri Aurobindo retired from daily interactions, and only The Mother had full access to him till the end of his life. The prohibition on outside visitors continued, except for a rare visit by Tagore in 1928. The only interaction with ashram inmates would be on darshan days—15 August and 24 November.

Sri Aurobindo did not consider himself to be a guru but ended up in an unusual and unconventional version of the role. He did not give instructions or a set of rules to be followed. He would guide the sadhaks through answers to questions put by them. This resulted in his spending a large part of time in answering a massive correspondence. A sample of this can be seen in the four huge volumes of *Letters on Yoga*. And they are just a selected fraction of what is actually available in the archives of the Ashram.

The Accident and After

On 24 November 1938, Sri Aurobindo got up at about 2 a.m. in the morning and walked across to his bathroom. He stumbled over a tiger skin pelt, which had been gifted to him. He tried to get up but was unable to, so he just lay there waiting for someone to come. The Mother came in, saw him and immediately

---

[160]*Complete Works of Sri Aurobindo: Volume 35: Letters on Himself and the Ashram,* Sri Aurobindo Ashram, 1997, p. 272.
[161]Ibid.

summoned help. When the doctors came, it was discovered that Sri Aurobindo had fractured the left thigh, close to the knee.

The Mother placed Ambulal Purani, Nirodbaran (a doctor) and Champklal on shifts to look after Sri Aurobindo. These were inspired choices, as being educated and curious people, both Purani and Nirodbaran were able to have conversations with Sri Aurobindo and elicit valuable information on his life, his yoga, spiritual experiences and the events of the day. In the case of Nirodbaran, there was also regular correspondence, which gives us some idea of Sri Aurobindo's humour. A pattern of evening talks commenced, which continued well into the Second World War years.

Sri Aurobindo was completely opposed to Hitler and was unable to understand those Indians who showed sympathy or support towards the Nazis and Imperial Japan simply because they were the enemies of India's rulers. He queried, 'How can they have sympathy for Hitler who is destroying other nations, taking away their liberty? It is not only pro-Ally sympathy but sympathy for humanity that they are jeering at.' And again, 'How can India, who wants freedom, take sides with somebody who takes away freedom from other nations?'[162] Sri Aurobindo had no doubt that the Axis powers would be ultimately defeated.

---

[162]Purani, A.B., *Evening Talks with Sri Aurobindo*, Sri Aurobindo Ashram, 2007.

10

Outside, Looking In (1910–47)

There has been a constant myth that as soon as Sri Aurobindo reached Pondicherry, he not only severed all his links with politics, but he also gave up all interest in politics and the world outside, preferring to spend his time perfecting his Integral Yoga. The reality was vastly different. Sri Aurobindo kept away from active politics but always kept abreast of the state of affairs. He had a number of private meetings with politicians before his seclusion. He made two public political interventions during the Second World War and sent private envoys to Congress leaders. In his last years, he closely looked at India's neighbourhood. Sri Aurobindo's last major public comment was on the state of the new Indian Union.

Past Links

While Sri Aurobindo refused to meet people from outside the ashram, the prohibition did not extend to old political associates, who visited him until realizing that he really had no interest in a return to active political life, their visits diminishing over time. However, after the end of hostilities in Europe, among the prominent visitors were Lala Lajpat Rai and B.S. Moonje. However, little information is available about their conversations.

Another link to the past was Annie Besant. Ironically, the

Home Rule leader had, during Sri Aurobindo's political years, been hostile to him and his advocacy. In 1909, shortly after his release, she had written about him:

> I see that some Indian papers resent what I said about Mr Arabinda Ghosh. I paid him the highest compliment of for purity of motive and patriotism in comparing him to Mazzini, one of the noblest men of the nineteenth century; but his bitter hatred of the English, and his refusal to work with any Englishman, however much a lover of India, mark him as fanatical; and his throwing of boys into political strife will ever have my opposition. He appears to have changed his tone much since his release, and though this may make him less popular with Extremists, it will make him more useful.[163]

The same Besant had no reservations about asking him to make a contribution to her paper, *New India*. Sri Aurobindo made two rarely noticed contributions in 1918, which were political in nature, and are the last explicitly political writings of his until the Second World War. The first was published in April, and linked national education and the Home Rule movement. Sri Aurobindo wrote:

> National Education is, next to Self-Government and along with it, the deepest and most immediate need of the country, and it is a matter of rejoicing for one to whom and earlier effort in that gave the first opportunity for identifying himself with the larger life and hope of the nation, to see the idea, for a time submerged, moving so soon towards self-fulfilment.[164]

---

[163]Besant, Annie, *The Central Hindu College Magazine*, vol. 9, 1909.
[164]*Complete Works of Sri Aurobindo: Volume 36: Autobiographical Notes and Other Writings of Historical Interest*, Sri Aurobindo Ashram, 1997, p. 270.

The second contribution was written as a letter to Besant, who had asked Sri Aurobindo for his views on the Montagu–Chelmsford proposals for Council reforms. After she received it, Besant asked for permission to publish the letter, to which Sri Aurobindo readily agreed. The letter was published in August and attributed to a nationalist. Eight years after his last foray into tilting at the windmills of the Raj, Sri Aurobindo once more rode into battle. Any reader familiar with his earlier writings would have instantly recognized the ironic style, which could have been used by only one person. Sri Aurobindo wrote: 'It can only be regarded as unwise by those who are always ready to take any shadow,—how much more a bulky and imposing shadow like this,—and are careless of the substance.'[165] Sri Aurobindo insisted that there was no real power in the system, and the whole affair was an eyewash.

The Baptista and Moonje Letters

In 1919, Joseph Baptista, a lawyer in Bombay who had been a strong supporter of Tilak, alongwith with a few other nationalists, decided to start a new radical party and a newspaper to spread its ideas. Baptista wrote to Sri Aurobindo, asking him to head the new paper.

Sri Aurobindo let Baptista down gently. He began his reply of 5 January 1920 with, 'Your offer is a tempting one, but I regret that I cannot answer it in the affirmative.' The first reason for declining Baptista's offer was, of course, the possibility that by returning to British India, he might have to 'waste my time in the leisured ease of an involuntary Governmemt guest.'[166] Then

---

[165]*Complete Works of Sri Aurobindo: Volume 8: Karmayogin*, Sri Aurobindo Ashram, 1997, p. 271.

[166]*Complete Works of Sri Aurobindo: Volume 36: Autobiographical Notes and Other Writings of Historical Interest*, Sri Aurobindo Ashram, 1997, p. 254.

he confessed that even if he had freedom of action, he still would not leave Pondicherry. 'I came to Pondicherry in order to have freedom and tranquilty for a fixed object having nothing to do with present politics...and until it is done it is not possible for me to resume any kind of political activity.' Then, in an evocative phrase, he described Pondicherry as his 'cave of tapsya' and that until he had finished his spiritual work here, there was no question of leaving. Sri Aurobindo then declared that, 'There is to me nothing secular, all human activity is for me a thing to be included in a completely spiritual life, and the importance of politics at the present time is very great.' He then said that he had come into politics with a certain determination—'to get into the mind of the people a settled will for freedom and the necessity of a struggle to achieve it.' That work, as the Amritsar session of the Congress indicated, was done. Moreover, he had a certain idea for how the future politics should be, and it would probably be out of step with the general will.

Then suddenly, Sri Aurobindo found himself stuck with an invitation from B.S. Moonje to head the Congress itself in its Nagpur session! He moved swiftly to stop the move, with a telegram declining the offer. He then, as in the case of Baptista, wrote a gracious letter on 30 August 1920 to Moonje, explaining the reasons for declining an invitation most people would have grabbed with both hands. He pointed out that he could not sign the Congress creed, as his own was very different. Moonje may well have been puzzled by an answer based on ethics, coming from such a legendary politician.

Sri Aurobindo then stressed the primary reason for his reluctance:

> The central reason, however, is this that I am no longer first and foremost a politician, but have definitely commenced another kind of work with a spiritual basis, a work of

spiritual, social, cultural and economic reconstruction of an almost revolutinary kind, am even making or at least supervising a sort of practical or laboratory experiment in that sense which needs all the attention and energy that I can have to spare.[167]

Sri Aurobindo made it clear that it was not possible for him to walk away from his sadhana in Pondicherry. He then pointed out that it was impossible for anyone, least of all himself, to take up the standard of Tilak. Only a Tilak would have been capable of that.

Sri Aurobindo then ended his letter with what can only be described as words of encouragement, in his inmitable style:

Might I suggest that the success of the Congress can hardly depend on the presence of a single person and one who has long been in obscurity? The friends who call on me are surely wrong in thinking that the Nagpur Congress will be uninspiring without me. The national movement is surely strong enough now to be inspired wih its own idea especially at a time of stress like the present.[168]

With these two letters, whose contents became public very quickly, Sri Aurobindo increased his mystique and at the same time, brought the curtain down firmly on any chance of a return to public life.

The Gandhian Moment

While Sri Aurobindo understood and accepted that Mahatma Gandhi was the principal leader of the nationalist movement after the First World War, he differed with Gandhi's strategy and tactics time and again.

---

[167]Ibid. 257.
[168]Ibid.

Gandhi, in South Africa, was working out his ideas of satyagraha at approximately the same time that Sri Aurobindo was working out the constituents of passive resistance. Here, the biggest difference between Gandhi and Sri Aurobindo was on non-violence. Aurobindo had at the time written:

> To submit to illegal and violent methods of coercion, to accept outrage and hooliganism as part of the legal procedures of the country is to be guilty of cowardice, and, by dwarfing national manhood, to sin against the divinity within ourselves and the divinity in our motherland. The moment of this kind is attempted, passive resistance ceases and active resistance becomes a duty.[169]

Gandhi sent his son, Devdas, to meet Sri Aurobindo in 1934. The visit was a shambles. After Devdas expounded on non-violence, Sri Aurobindo asked him, 'Suppose there is an invasion of India by the Afghans, how are you going to meet it with non-violence?' Devdas had no answer. An apocryphal story goes that Devdas saw Sri Aurobindo smoking a cigar and asked why he was attached to cigars. Sri Aurobindo immediately retored, 'Why are you so attached to non-attachment?'

Gandhi made several futile bids to meet Sri Aurobindo, receiving an answer always in the negative. Gandhi wrote, saying that ever since he had returned from South Africa, he had wanted to meet Sri Aurobindo. Sri Aurobindo wrote back in his own hand, regretting that he could not bend his rule of not meeting people even for the Mahatma. Gandhi did not try to wrangle an invitation again. When Gandhi came to Pondicherry, he avoided going near the ashram, fearing that he might be forced to meet Sri Aurobindo. In the event, they never met.

---

[169] *Complete Works of Sri Aurobindo, Volume 6: Bande Mataram — I–II*, Sri Aurobindo Ashram, 1997, p. 294.

The Second World War and After

Sri Aurobindo, as we have seen earlier, was supportive of the Allied cause. He was not happy when the Congress ministers resigned en masse from office after the Viceroy had failed to consult them before declaring war against the Axis powers.

Sri Aurobindo sent 10,000 francs to the French Defence Fund and Rs. 1000 to the Viceroy's War fund immediately after the collapse of France. Sri Aurobindo shocked the Indian political world when, in September 1940, he publicly donated Rs. 500 to the Governor of Madras' War Fund. In a public message, he said:

> We feel that not only is this a battle waged in just self-defence and in defence of the nations threatened with the world-domination of Germany and the Nazi system of life, but that it is a defence of civilisation and its highest attained social, cultural and spiritual values and of the whole future of humanity. To this cause our support and sympathy will be unswerving whatever may happen; we look forward to the victory of Britain, and as the eventual result, an era of peace and union among the nations and a better and more secure world-order.[170]

Two years later, an extraordinary move was undertaken by Sri Aurobindo. In his second intervention in the war effort, he welcomed the offer of Sir Stafford Cripps in 1942 for Indian participation in the Government of India minus the defence portfolio, with a Constituent Assembly at the end of the war. He wrote a tetter to Cripps, in which he said:

> As one who has been a nationalist leader and worker for India's independence though now my activity is no longer in

---

[170]*Complete Works of Sri Aurobindo: Volume 36: Autobiographical Notes and Other Writings of Historical Interest*, Sri Aurobindo Ashram, 1997, p. 453.

the political but in the spiritual field, I wish to express my appreciaton of all you have done to bring about this offer... I hope that it will be accepted and the right use made of it putting aside all discords and divisions.[171]

Sri Aurobindo encouraged the Congress to accept the offer, as he believed it gave India something just short of independence. He sent Duraiswami Iyer, a lawyer from Madras with political connections, to Delhi to press upon the leadership of the Congress to accept the Cripps offer without delay. Indians would have control of all but one ministry. If necessary, they could stop all work. Sri Aurobindo also sent telegrams to Moonje and C. Rajagopalachari, a senior leader from Madras, that they should accept the offer immediately.

Similarly, when the Wavell Plan was unveiled, he urged that it be accepted, saying that, in some ways, it was better than the Cripps offer, though he decried the communal basis for the formation of the government by the Congress and Muslim League. No formal statement was made for the Cabinet Mission plan, but it was clear that Sri Aurobindo accepted all these plans, as they put India on the road to independence.

---

[171]Ibid. 468.

11
Twilight (1947–50)

The independence of India was the goal that Sri Aurobindo had set for himself as a boy in England. After his departure into exile, he had made a public declaration that it would come soon. However, he could not have foreseen that it would be accompanied by the violent partition of India, and that a terrible price would have to be paid by people of all communities, though he had warned of such a possibility.

Indpendence

Sri Aurobindo, as one of the stalwarts of the early nationalist movement, and the man who had specifically called for Indian independence, was asked to make a statement to be broadcast on the eve of the great day. Sri Aurobindo believed that the fact that independence came on his birthday—15 August—was a divinely ordained command. The message as written was deemed to be too long and so was edited down.

Sri Aurobindo spoke of his vision for the future at three levels—India, Asia and the world. At each level, he saw a unification taking place. 'India is free but she has not achieved unity, only a fissured and broken freedom. At one time, it almost seemed as if she might relapse into the chaos of separate states... The wise drastic policy of the Constituent Assembly makes it possible that the problem of the depressed classes will be solved without schism or fissure.'[172] He sadly notes, 'the old communal division into Hindu and Muslim seems to have hardened into the figure of a permanent political division of the country.' It should not be accepted as a permanent fact, but the country should be reunited in some way, 'For without it the destiny of India might be seriously impaired and even frustrated.'

Asia, he noted, was in a transitional phase—parts of it had overthrown the foreign yoke, others were in the process of delinking from their colonial masters, yet others were still unfree. However, Sri Aurobindo believed that it was only a matter of time till the whole of Asia was free. He said that, 'There India has her part to play and has begun to play it with an energy and ability which already indicate the measure of her possibilities and the place she can take in the council of the nations.'[173]

Sri Aurobindo proclaimed that 'The unification of Mankind is under way, though only in an imperfect initiative, organised but struggling against tremendous difficulties.' But there already was a movement in that direction, and he believed that in this, too, India had a tremendous role to play. The presence of India or its absence could be the difference between a slow or a quick development. 'A new spirit of oneness will take hold of the human race,' Sri Aurobindo wrote.[174]

He added that 'The spiritual gift of India to the world has already begun. India's spirituality is entering Europe and America in an ever increasing measure. That movement will grow, amid the disasters of the time more and more eyes are turning towards her with hope and there is even an increasing resort not only to her teachings, but to her psychic and spiritual practice.'[175]

---

[172]Ibid. 474.
[173]Ibid.
[174]Ibid.
[175]Ibid.

He noted that there were great difficulties in the way, but they could be overcome with the spirit of willingness. 'Here too, if this evolution is to take place, since it must come through a growth of the spirit and the inner consciousness, the initiative can come from India and although the scope must be universal, the central movement may be hers.'[176]

Linguistic Provinces

Sri Aurobindo had, as a rule, refused to accept any honours or prizes from governments. He was put into a fix when Andhra University asked him if he would be willing to receive the C.R. Reddy National Prize. The honour did not break his rules, and they had also agreed to hold a special convocation at the ashram in Pondicherry, thus removing the necessity of Sri Aurobindo having to travel elsewhere to receive the award. Sri Aurobindo agreed and the award was presented in December 1948.

One of the reasons that Sri Aurobindo had agreed appears to have been that the event gave him a certain platform to speak publicly on a subject that exercised his mind and agitated the mind of the public and was very much in the public eye— linguistic states. Sri Aurobindo, of course, had been asked to write something linked to Andhra.

Sri Aurobindo noted that the biggest political issue in India at the time was the demand for the reconfiguration of the British presidencies and provinces into more viable states created on a linguistic basis. As Sri Aurobindo put it 'the demand for the reconstruction of the artificial British-made Presidencies and Provinces into natural divisions forming a new system, new and yet found founded on the principle of diversity in unity attempted by ancient India.'[177]

---

[176]Ibid.
[177]Ibid. 498.

According to Sri Aurobindo, the Himalayas and the Indian Ocean had created a peculiar people with distinct characteristics of theirs, with their own civilization welded into a fundamental unity. However, political unity had eluded them, and it created a 'congeries of diverse peoples, lands, kingdoms and in earlier times, republics also, diverse races, sub-nations with a marked character of their own, developing different brands or forms of civilisation and cultue, many schools of art and architecture which yet succeeded in fitting into the general Indian type of civilisation.'[178]

The tendency throughout Indian history, said Sri Aurobindo, was an effort to bind all these diverse elements under a central imperial rule so that the cultural unity was matched by a political unity. But this political unity was never attained, and remained elusive till the arrival of the British. They made provinces in a way that served their own interests, in the process, creating huge multilinguistic and multi-ethnic entities. These continued into the present day and threatened to become permanent, after crushing all the differences and creating an artificial unity.

Some people, according to Sri Aurobindo, wanted a unification, which is uniformity: 'In a rigorous unification they see the only true union, a single nation with a standardized and uniform administration, language, literature, culture, art, education—all carried on through the agency of one national tongue. How far such a conception can be carried out in the future one cannot forecast, but at present it is obviously impracticable, and it is doubtful if it is for India truly desirable.'[179]

Sri Aurobindo pointed out that while these diversities had in the past posed problems, they had also been responsible for the rich creativity displayed in all areas of life. According to Sri

---

[178]Ibid.
[179]Ibid.

Aurobindo, the Congress had, prior to Independence, promised the creation of such linguistic states, and should adhere to it, as the alternative could be worse. As such, 'India's national life will then be founded on her natural strengths and the principle of unity in diversity which has always been normal to her and its fulfillment the fundamental course of her being and its very nature, the Many in the One, would place her on the sure foundation of her Swabhava and Swadharma.'[180]

Sri Aurobindo then turned to the question of what the future holds, and the role that universities could play: 'In this hour, in the second year of its liberation the nation has to awaken to many more very considerable problems, to vast possibilities opening before her but also to dangers and dangers that may, if not wisely dealt with, become formidable.' There was a danger of India becoming like all others and losing her spiritual insight, at a time when the whole world was turning to it. This was to be avoided at all costs, and the danger had to be always kept in sight.[181]

Savitri

Savitri is the poem that the poet in Sri Aurobindo was born to write. He first came across the legend of Savitri and Satyavan in his Baroda days, while reading the Mahabharata. He refers to it approvingly in his 'Notes on the Mahabharatha', written in about 1901. It is said that he began work on it in Baroda, but if that was so, no manuscript has survived.

The earliest known manuscript is from Pondicherry, dated 8/9 August 1916. Sri Aurobindo worked on it intermittently till the early 1920s. Work resumed on it in 1931 and continued

---

[180]Ibid.
[181]Ibid.

intermittently. When Sri Aurobindo's eyesight began to fail in the 1940s, he began to dictate and revise it. He finally completed it just a few months before his death. The 1993 edition of *Savitri* has a total of 23,837 lines.

What is *Savitri*? At one level, it is a recreation of one of the best-known stories from the Mahabharata, but throroughly Aurobindoized. At another level, it is a kind of spiritual autobiography. After all, in 1947, Sri Aurobindo wrote to Amal Kiran, 'I used *Savitri* as a means of ascencion. I began with it on a certain mental level, each time I could reach a higher level I rewrote from that level...'[182] At yet another level, it can be approached as an entry into the Integral Yoga of Sri Aurobindo. Its length and subject have left modern critics cold, but anyone who plunges into its depth understands that this is a masterpiece.

The Supramental Manifestation

The Mother had started a school, and later it began to issue a journal. The Mother asked Sri Aurobindo to write for it, and he gave a seven-part series titled 'The Supramental Manifestation'. The series is incomplete and comprises Sri Aurobindo's last writings. It can be said to be a supplement to *The Life Divine*. It explores the possibility of the continued evolution of the body and introduces the concept of the 'Mind of Light'. According to Sri Aurobindo, this is a mind that no longer seeks knowledge in ignorance, but a mind that can live in Truth, is capable of being Truth-conscious and living a direct rather than an indirect knowledge.

---

[182]*Complete Works of Sri Aurobindo: Volume 33–34: Savitri—A Legend and a Symbol,* Sri Aurobindo Ashram, 1997.

China and Tibet

Sri Aurobindo continued to be a canny observer of the national and international political scene. When China invaded Tibet, K.D. Sethna (Amal Kiran) wrote an editorial, the contents of which had been dictated by Sri Aurobindo: 'The basic significance of Mao's Tibetan adventure is to advance China's frontiers right down to India and stand poised there to strike at the right moment and with the right strategy...'[183] Sri Aurobindo proved prescient, when China did indeed attack India in 1962.

The Passing of a Giant

Sri Aurobindo weakned physically after his accident but still managed largely on his own. But he later developed a kidney infection and prostaic enlargement. He began to withdraw from people, giving brief or monosyllabic answers. On 24 November, darshan was concluded hurriedly at his request. A blood test on 4 December indicated immiment kidney failure. He called Nirodbaran at 11 p.m. and had a sip of water. The Mother came at midnight, and they exchanged a look. Shortly after, at about 1.26 a.m., Sri Aurobindo passed away. Sri Aurobindo was laid to rest in a tomb in the ashram premises on 9 December. The great journey was over. As Sri Aurobindo wrote in *Savitri*:

> *A pilgrim of the everlasting truth,*
> *Our measures cannot hold his measureless mind;*
> *He has turned from the voices of the narrow realm*
> *And left the little lane of human Time.*

---

[183]Iyengar, K.R. Srinivasa, *Sri Aurobindo: A Biography and a History*, Sri Aurobindo Centre of Education, 1972, p. 696.

12
New Yoga, New World, New India

The last 40 years of Sri Aurobindo's life were spent in Pondicherry, which, in a memorable phrase in his letter to Joseph Baptista, he had called his 'cave of tapasya'. During the period when he was working on the *Arya*, he wrote all the books that form the bedrock of Integral Yoga, as well as his ruminations on the future of international society and a template for a future India derived from its past. It is important to remember that for Sri Aurobindo, all life was yoga. Which means that for Sri Aurobindo, all life was a part of his spiritual enterprise.

Integral Yoga

The Life Divine and *The Synthesis of Yoga* are the principal works in which Sri Aurobindo made his exposition of Integral Yoga. It must be noted that neither of the two is a finished work. They both first appeared in the *Arya*, and were extensively revised before publication in book form. Sri Aurbindo's death prevented their completion.

In *The Life Divine*, Sri Aurobindo explains how life on earth can be divinized. It requires close reading and is at times difficult to understand because of the almost technical nature of the language. The following discussion is a somewhat simplified version of its philosophical vision. It is also imperative to understand that

The Life Divine is not philosophy in the usual sense but spiritual philosophy. The inspirational sources indicate that Sri Aurobindo is retracing a path that was once known, perhaps only partially, and then lost. Whether it is the Bhagavad Gita or the Upanishads, these sources indicate that only shards of the original knowledge have survived.

In essence, we can say that a Divine Godhead has created the Universe, and we are all its creations. Inconscience and inanimatedness are the initial seeds of existence. However, within them lie the process through which they evolve from Matter to Life to Mind over a period of millennia. But the Mind has only a fragmentary understanding, and continues to evolve through different levels of consciousness, until it reaches the supramental consciousness, which enables us to live a divine life on Earth. It is important to note that the yoga of Sri Aurobindo does not aim at either a souless materiality or a transcendental bliss, but a life of bliss and joy, right here on Earth.

The individual evolves through incarnation. Through each lifetime, new understandings are known, until the individual realizes what its true destiny is and actively aspires for it, leading to the creation of a perfected body. As Sri Aurobindo observes, 'The body will be turned by the power of the spiritual consciousness into a true and fit and perfectly responsive instrument of the Spirit. This new relation of the spirit and the body assumes—and makes possible—a free acceptance of the whole of material Nature in place of a rejection.'[184] If enough individuals tread this sunlit path, then a transformation of society worldwide is possible, where truth, harmony, love and beauty will predominate.

The Life Divine is one part of the overall understanding of Integral Yoga. *The Synthesis of Yoga* is the 'How To' part, as it

---

[184]*Complete Works of Sri Aurobindo: Volume 22: The Life Divine—I–II*, Sri Aurobindo Ashram, 1997, p. 1021.

were, without any actual instructions for practice, as is usual in most paths of yoga. The first three parts of the book take an Aurobindian look at the traditional yogas of the Bhagavad Gita, a seed text for Sri Aurobindo's Integral Yoga, which is discussed in the fourth part. Integral Yoga is also known as the Yoga of Integral Perfection, which is also a chapter that essentially summarizes what Sri Aurobindo had written in the main part of the book.

Sri Aurobindo, in a 1934 essay tittled 'Sri Aurobindo's Teaching', summarizes the first three sections thus:

> There are many things belonging to older systems that are necessary on the way—an opening of the mind to a greater wideness and to the sense of the Self and the Infinite, an emergence into what has been called the cosmic consciousness, mastery over the desires and passions; an outward asceticism is not essential, but the conquest of desire and attachment and a control over the body and its needs, greeds and instincts is indispensable. There is a combination of the old systems: the way of knowledge through the mind's discernment between Reality and the appearance, the heart's way of devotion, love and surrender and the way of works turning the will away from motives of self-interest to the Truth and the service of a greater Reality than the ego. For the whole being has to be trained so that it can respond and be transformed when it is possible for that greater Light and Force to work in the nature.[185]

Transcendent Internationalism

The Ideal of Human Unity and *The Human Cycle* are, in a way, Sri Aurobindo's contribution to the theory of social development

[185]*Complete Works of Sri Aurobindo: Volume 36: Autobiographical Notes and Other Writings of Historical Interest*, Sri Aurobindo Ashram, 1997, p. 547.

and the evolution of international society.

In *The Ideal of Human Unity*, Sri Aurobindo tried to use the data of history to try and predict what conditions could possibly result in uniting humankind peacefully. He realized that a rigid unification of nations could lead to a global despoticracy. Therefore, he sought ways in which the freedom of individuals could be preserved, resulting in a global society in which the individual can flourish, thus leading to social happiness and prosperity.

In *The Human Cycle*, Sri Aurobindo, basing himself upon the theories of a German historian Karl Lamprecht, attempted to construct a typology for Indian history. The Vedic Age was termed the Symbolic Age: 'The religious institution of sacrifice governs the whole society and all its hours and moments, and the ritual of the sacrifice is at every turn and in every detail mystically symbolic.'

The next was the Typal Age, which was 'predominantly psychological and ethical... Religion becomes then a mystic sanction for the ethical motive and diisciplne...This Typal stage creates the great social ideals which remain impressed upon the human age even when the stage itself is passed.'[186]

The next is the Conventional Age, where all ideals are distorted, and the external and superficial dominates, such as the caste system. The Individualistic Age, as in Europe, deepens democratic rights. This is followed by the Subjective Age, when humanity begins to examine itself and starts to look beyond the external. Finally, the Gnostic Age arises, where, essentially, the supramental prevails and humanity is guided by the Divine Light.

---

[186]*Complete Works of Sri Aurobindo: Volume 25: The Human Cycle—The Ideal of Human Unity—War and Self-Determination*, Sri Aurobindo Ashram, 1997, p. 7.

New India in Old India

One of Sri Aurobindo's finest works was written in the *Arya* as a counterblast to William Archer's book *India and the Future*. It features all the elements of the style which had made his name back in the day—sarcasm, humour, irony and the deployment of a vast reservoir of knowledge. Additionally, it has a little bit of the disapproving tone that is adopted by someone a little irked the display of half-baked information. Archer had written a book in which he had questioned whether India could, in any way whatsoever, be called civilized, and whether it had any culture worth speaking of. It had drawn a mild reproof from John Woodroffe, the tantric expert, in his book *Is India Civilized?* It now drew the wrath of Aurobindo, who trained his guns on it in a series of articles published in the *Arya* with the overall title 'A Defence of Indian Culture'.

Sri Aurobindo refuted Archer with a definition of the cultural history of India. He ranged across Indian spirituality and life, art, literature and polity. He, at one point, asked a question, which immediately makes Sri Aurobindo our contemporary:

> Why are a certain class of Indians still hypnotized in all fields by European culture and why are we at all still hypnotized by it in the field of politics? Because they constantly saw all the power, creation, activity on the side of Europe, all the immobility or weakness of a static inefficient defence on the side of India. But wherever the Indian spirit has been able to react, to attack with energy and to create with éclat, the European glamour has begun immediately to lose its hypnotic power.[187]

---

[187]*Complete Works of Sri Aurobindo: Volume 20: The Renaissance in India with A Defence of Indian Culture*, Sri Aurobindo Ashram, 1997, p. 62.

Edward Said could not have put it better. Every one of Sri Aurobindo's rebuttal of Archer is laced with one principal motif—that it is India's unique spiritual heritage that is present in every part of its civilization, whether it is architecture, literature or politics. Sri Aurobindo points out how the old, ancient culture is capable and worthy of being the foundation for a new modern Indian culture, designed by her own people.

We end with Sri Aurobindo's prophetic message for New India from Old India:

> India of the ages is not dead nor has she spoken her last creative word; she lives and has still something to do for herself and the human peoples. And that which must seek now to awake is not an anglicised oriental people, docile pupil of the West and doomed to repeat the cycle of the occident's success and failure, but still the ancient immemorable Shakti recovering her deepest self, lifting her head higher towards the supreme source of light and strength and turning to discover the complete meaning and a vaster form of her Dharma.[188]

---

[188]Ibid. 444.

Epilogue
The Sunlit Path

The news of the death of Sri Aurobindo was published across India and in other parts of the world. Tributes poured in from across political lines in India, led by Prime Minister Jawaharlal Nehru. As a teenager in England, Nehru used to read Sri Aurobindo's political writings, which had been sent to him by his father, Motilal Nehru.

However, Sri Aurobindo's prominence began to dim over time, as the the nationalist movement receded into the past. The philosophical and spiritual writings became subjects of study in academe, much of it ephemereal, some of it of continued interest. The ashram continued to develop under The Mother, and is at the heart of Pondicherry today. Outside academe, Sri Aurobindo was seen as a distant spiritual leader and was respected in a formal way. His political writings were deemed to be of relevance to his time only. Sri Aurobindo, in short, was seen as a historical figure of niche interest. The principal aim of *Mystic Fire* has been to rescue Sri Aurobindo from this undeserved historical obscurity and relocate this remarkable life in modern Indian history. The secondary aim is to point out that his writings have a surprising level of relevance to India today and in the future. For Sri Aurobindo's work is not a dead letter but a living, provocative mass of ideas.

A constant hinderance in the study of Sri Aurobindo's nationalism has been the charge of communal bias against non-Hindus, a charge that we have seen to be unfounded. Sri Aurobindo's idea of Indian nationalism was wide and inclusive, and not the narrow Hindu nationalism of V.D. Savarkar. It is this Indian nationalism, drawing upon the ancient past, but not being overwhelmed by it, which needs its place in the sun. The base of Sri Aurobindo's politics, which can be the base for political renewal today, was ethical in nature. He stressed a level of political selflessness, which is not seen or heard today. These are important lessons we can draw from the life and works of Sri Aurobindo for India of the twentieth century.

A key element in the thought of Sri Aurobindo's life and work—political, spiritual, philosophical and poetical—is evolution. Sri Aurobindo taught that everything changes, nothing remains the same. When he reached back into the past, it was not to reproduce it. It was to examine it, remove all that was obscure or redundant, and present it to us as a living, vital element for our lives in this century.

All of Sri Aurobindo's teachings have human beings at its centre. The human being will evolve, at the personal, community and global levels, transcending all limitations of community and national boundaries. Everything that Sri Aurobindo worked for is the liberation of human beings. Freedom was the core thought of Sri Aurobindo. Only when the individual is free, social and national progress can take place. As Sri Aurobindo wrote: 'The free individual is the conscious progressive: it is only when he is able to impart his own creative and mobile consciousness to the mass that a progressive society becomes possible.'[189]

Sri Aurobindo worked for the freedom of the individual, the nation and the world. It is the importance and necessity of freedom that is the most important lesson from Sri Aurobindo for us today.

---

[189]*Complete Works of Sri Aurobindo: Volume 25: The Human Cycle—The Ideal of Human Unity—War and Self-Determination*, Sri Aurobindo Ashram, 1997, p. 512.

Appendix I

Sri Aurobindo's Uttarpara speech, dated 30 May 1909. The text was thoroughly revised and published in Karmayogin *on 19 and 26 June.*

When I was asked to speak to you at the annual meeting of your Sabha, it was my intention to say a few words about the subject chosen for today, the subject of the Hindu religion. I do not know now whether I shall fulfil that intention; for as I sat here, there came into my mind a word that I have to speak to you, a word that I have to speak to the whole of the Indian Nation. It was spoken first to myself in jail and I have come out of jail to speak it to my people.

It was more than a year ago that I came here last. When I came I was not alone; one of the mightiest prophets of Nationalism (= Bepin Pal) sat by my side. It was he who then came out of the seclusion to which God had sent him, so that in the silence and solitude of his cell he might hear the word that He had to say. It was he that you came in your hundreds to welcome. Now he is far away, separated from us by thousands of miles. Others whom I was accustomed to find working beside me are absent. The storm that swept over the country has scattered them far and wide. It is I this time who have spent one year in seclusion, and now that I come out I find all changed. One who always sat by my side and was associated in my work is a prisoner in Burma; another is in the north rotting in detention. I looked round when I came out, I looked round for those to whom I had been accustomed to look for counsel and inspiration. I did not find them. There was more than that. When I went to jail the whole country was alive with the cry of Bande Mataram, alive with the hope of a nation, the hope of millions of men who had newly risen out of degradation. When I came out of jail I listened for that cry, but there was instead a silence. A hush had fallen on the country and men seemed bewildered; for instead of God's bright heaven full of the vision of the future that had been before us, there seemed to be overhead a leaden sky from which human thunders and lightnings rained. No man seemed to know which way to move, and from all sides came the question, 'What shall we do next? What is there that we can do ?' I too did not know which way to move, I too did not know what was next to be done. But one thing I knew, that as it was the Almighty Power of God which had raised that cry, that hope, so it was the same Power which had sent down that silence. He who was in the shouting and the movement was also in the pause and the hush. He has sent it upon us, so that the nation might draw back for a moment and look into itself and know His will. I have not been disheartened by that silence because I had been made familiar with silence in my prison and because I knew it was in the pause and the hush that I had myself learned this lesson through the long year of my detention. When Bepin Chandra Pal came out of jail, he came with a message, and it was an inspired message. I remember the speech he made here. It was a speech not so much political as religious in its bearing and intention. He spoke of his realisation in jail, of God within us all, of the Lord within the nation, and in his subsequent speeches also he spoke of a greater than ordinary force in the movement and a greater than ordinary purpose before it. Now I also meet you again, I also come out of jail, and again it is you of Uttarpara who are the first to welcome me, not at a political meeting but at a meeting of a society for the protection of our religion. That message which Bepin Chandra Pal received in Buxar jail, God gave to me in Alipore. That knowledge He gave to me day after day during my twelve months of imprisonment and it is that which He has commanded me to speak to you now that I have come out.

I knew I would come out. The year of detention was meant only for a year of seclusion and of training. How could anyone hold me in jail longer than was necessary for God's purpose ? He had given me a word to speak and a work to do, and until that word was spoken I knew that no human power could hush me, until that work was done no human power could stop God's instrument, however weak that instrument might be or however small. Now that I have come out, even in these few minutes, a word has been suggested to me which I had no wish to speak. The thing I had in my mind He has thrown from it and what I speak is under an impulse and a compulsion.

When I was arrested and hurried to the Lal Bazar hajat I was shaken in faith for a while, for I could not look into the heart of His intention. Therefore I faltered for a moment and cried out in my heart to Him, 'What is this that has happened to me? I believed that I had a mission to work for the people of my country and until that work was done, I should have Thy protection. Why then am I here and on such a charge?' A day passed and a second day and a third, when a voice came to me from within, 'Wait and see.' Then I grew calm and waited, I was taken from Lal Bazar to Alipore and was placed for one month in a solitary cell apart from men. There I waited day and night for the voice of God within me, to know what He had to say to me, to learn what I had to do. In this seclusion the earliest realisation, the first lesson came to me. I remembered then that a month or more before my arrest, a call had come to me to put aside all activity, to go in seclusion and to look into myself, so that I might enter into closer communion with Him. I was weak and could not accept the call. My work was very dear to me and in the pride of my heart I thought that unless I was there, it would suffer or even fail and cease; therefore I would not leave it. It seemed to me that He spoke to me again and said, 'The bonds you had not the strength to break, I have broken for you, because it is not my will nor was it ever my intention that that should continue. I have had another thing for you to do and it is for that I have brought you here, to teach you what you could not learn for yourself and to train you for my work.' Then He placed the Gita in my hands. His strength entered into me and I was able to do the sadhana of the Gita. I was not only to understand intellectually but to realise what Sri Krishna demanded of Arjuna and what He demands of those who aspire to do His work, to be free from repulsion and desire, to do work for Him without the demand for fruit, to renounce self-will and become a passive and faithful instrument in His hands, to have an equal heart for high and low, friend and opponent, success and failure, yet not to do His work negligently. I realised what the Hindu religion meant. We speak often of the Hindu religion, of the Sanatan Dharma, but few of us really know what that religion is. Other religions are preponderatingly religions of faith and profession, but the Sanatan Dharma is life itself; it is a thing that has not so much to be believed as lived. This is the Dharma that for the salvation of humanity was cherished in the seclusion of this peninsula from of old. It is to give this religion that India is rising. She does not rise as other countries do, for self or when she is strong, to trample on the weak. She is rising to shed the eternal light entrusted to her over the world. India has always existed for humanity and not for herself and it is for humanity and not for herself that she must be great.

Therefore this was the next thing He pointed out to me, - He made me realise the central truth of the Hindu religion. He turned the hearts of my jailors to me and they spoke to the Englishman in charge of the jail, 'He is suffering in his confinement; let him at least walk outside his cell for half an hour in the morning and in the evening.' So it was arranged, and it was while I was walking that His strength again entered into me. I looked the jail that secluded me from men and it was no longer by its high walls that I was imprisoned; no, it was Vasudeva who surrounded me. I walked under the branches of the tree in front of my cell but it was not the tree, I knew it was Vasudeva, it was Sri Krishna whom I saw standing there and holding over me his shade. I looked at the bars of my cell, the very grating that did duty for a door and again I saw Vasudeva. It was Narayana who was guarding and standing sentry over me. Or I lay on the coarse blankets that were given me for a couch and felt the arms of Sri Krishna around me, the arms of my Friend and Lover. This was the first use of the deeper vision He gave me. I looked at the prisoners in the jail, the thieves, the murderers, the swindlers, and as I looked at them I saw Vasudeva, it was Narayana whom I found in these darkened souls and misused bodies. Amongst these thieves and dacoits there were many who put me to shame by their sympathy, their kindness, the humanity triumphant over such adverse circumstances. One I saw among them especially, who seemed to me a saint, a peasant of my nation who did not know how to read and write, an alleged dacoit sentenced to ten years' rigorous imprisonment, one of those whom we look down upon in our Pharisaical pride of class as Chhotalok. Once more He spoke to me and said, 'Behold the people among whom I have sent you to do a little of my work. This is the nature of the nation I am raising up and the reason why I raise them.'

When the case opened in the lower court and we were brought before the Magistrate I was followed by the same insight. He said to me, 'When you were cast into jail, did not your heart fail and did you not cry out to me, where is Thy protection ? Look now at the Magistrate, look now at the Prosecuting Counsel.' I looked and it was not the Magistrate whom I saw, it was Vasudeva, it was Narayana who was sitting there on the bench. I looked at the Prosecuting Counsel and it was not the Counsel for the prosecution that I saw; it was Sri Krishna who sat there, it was my Lover and Friend who sat there and smiled. 'Now do you fear ?' He said, 'I am in all men and I overrule their actions and their words. My protection is still with you and you shall not fear. This case which is brought against you, leave it in my hand. It is not for you. It was not for the trial that I brought you here but for something else. The case itself is only a means for my work and nothing more.' Afterwards when the trial opened in the Sessions Court, I began to write many instructions for my Counsel as to what was false in the evidence against me and on what points the witnesses might be cross-examined. Then something happened which I had not expected. The arrangements which had been made for my defence were suddenly changed and another Counsel stood there to defend me. He came unexpectedly, - a friend of mine, but I did not know he was coming. You have all heard the name of the man who put away from him all other thoughts and abandoned all his practice, who sat up half the night day after day for months and broke his health to save me, - Srijut Chittaranjan Das. When I saw him, I was satisfied, but I still thought it necessary to write instructions. Then all that was put away from me and I had the message from within, 'This is the man who will save you from the snares put around your feet. Put aside those papers. It is not you who will instruct him. I will instruct him.' From that time I did not of myself speak a word to my Counsel about the case or give a single instruction, and if ever I was asked a question, I always found that my answer did not help the case. I had left it to him and he took it entirely into his hands, with what result you know. I knew all along what He meant for me, for I heard it again and again, always I listened to the voice within; 'I am guiding, therefore fear not. Turn to your own work for which I have brought you to jail and when you come out, remember never to fear, never to hesitate. Remember that it is I who am doing this, not you nor any other. Therefore whatever clouds may come, whatever dangers and sufferings, whatever difficulties, whatever impossibilities, there is nothing impossible, nothing difficult. I am in the nation and its uprising and I am Vasudeva, I am Narayana, and what I will, shall be, not what others will. What I choose to bring about, no human power can stay.'

Meanwhile He had brought me out of solitude and placed me among those who had been accused along with me. You have spoken much today of my self-sacrifice and devotion to my country. I have heard that kind of speech ever since I came out of jail, but I hear it with embarrassment, with something of pain. For I know my weakness, I am a prey to my own faults and backslidings. I was not blind to them before and when they all rose up against me in seclusion, I felt them utterly. I knew them that I the man was a man of weakness, a faulty and imperfect instrument, strong only when a higher strength entered into me. Then I found myself among these young men and in many of them I discovered a mighty courage, a power of self-effacement in comparison with which I was simply nothing. I saw one or two who were not only superior to me in force and character, - very many were that, - but in the promise of that intellectual ability on which I prided myself. He said to me, 'This is the young generation, the new and mighty nation that is arising at my command. They are greater than yourself. What have you to fear ? If you stood aside or slept, the work would still be done. If you were cast aside tomorrow, here are the young men who will take up your work and do it more mightily than you have ever done. You have only got some strength from me to speak a word to this nation which will help to raise it.' This was the next thing He told me.

Then a thing happened suddenly and in a moment I was hurried away to the seclusion of a solitary cell. What happened to me during that period I am not impelled to say, but only that day after day, He showed me His wonders and made me realise the utter truth of the Hindu religion. I had many doubts before. I was brought up in England amongst foreign ideas and an atmosphere entirely foreign. About many things in Hinduism I had once been inclined to believe that they were imaginations, that there was much of dream in it, much that was delusion and Maya. But now day after day I realised in the mind, I realised in the heart, I realised in the body the truths of the Hindu religion. They became living experiences to me, and things were opened to me which no material science could explain. When I first approached Him, it was not entirely in the spirit of the Jnani. I came to Him long ago in Baroda some years before the Swadeshi began and I was drawn into the public field.

When I approached God at that time, I hardly had a living faith in Him. The agnostic was in me, the atheist was in me, the sceptic was in me and I was not absolutely sure that there was a God at all. I did not feel His presence. Yet something drew me to the truth of the Vedas, the truth of the Gita, the truth of the Hindu religion. I felt there must be a mighty truth somewhere in this Yoga, a mighty truth in this religion based on the Vedanta. So when I turned to the Yoga and resolved to practise it and find out if my idea was right, I did it in this spirit and with this prayer to Him, 'If Thou art, then Thou knowest my heart. Thou knowest that I do not ask for Mukti, I do not ask for anything which others ask for. I ask only for strength to uplift this nation, I ask only to be allowed to live and work for this people whom I love and to whom I pray that I may devote my life.' I strove long for the realisation of Yoga and at last to some extent I had it, but in what I most desired I was not satisfied. Then in the seclusion of the jail, of the solitary cell I asked for it again. I said, 'Give

me Thy Adesh. I do not know what work to do or how to do it.
Give me a message.' In the communion of Yoga two messages
came. The first message said, 'I have given you a work and it is
to help to uplift this nation. Before long the time will come when
you will have to go out of jail; for it is not my will that this time
either you should be convicted or that you should pass the time, as
others have to do, in suffering for their country. I have called you
to work, and that is the Adesh for which you have asked. I give
you the Adesh to go forth and do my work.' The second message
came and it said, 'Something has been shown to you in this year
of seclusion, something about which you had your doubts and
it is the truth of the Hindu religion. It is this religion that I am
raising up before the world, it is this that I have perfected and
developed through the Rishis, saints and Avatars, and now it is
going forth to do my work among the nations. I am raising up this
nation to send forth my word. This is the Sanatan Dharma, this
is the eternal religion which you did not really know before, but
which I have now revealed to you. The agnostic and the sceptic
in you have been answered, for I have given you proofs within
and without you, physical and subjective, which have satisfied
you. When you go forth, speak to your nation always this word,
that it is for the Sanatan Dharma that they arise, it is for the
world and not for themselves that they arise. I am giving them
freedom for the service of the world. When therefore it is said
that India shall rise, it is the Sanatan Dharma that shall be great.
When it is said that India shall expand and extend herself, it is
the Sanatan Dharma that shall expand and extend itself over
the world. It is for the Dharma and by the Dharma that India
exists. To magnify the religion means to magnify the country. I
have shown you that I am everywhere and in all men and in all
things, that I am in this movement and I am not only working
in those who are striving for the country but I am working also
in those who oppose them and stand in their path. I am working

in everybody and whatever men may think or do, they can do nothing but help in my purpose. They also are doing my work, they are not my enemies but my instruments. In all your actions you are moving forward without knowing which way you move. You mean to do one thing and you do another. You aim at a result and your efforts subserve one that is different or contrary. It is Shakti that has gone forth and entered into the people. Since long ago I have been preparing this uprising and now the time has come and it is I who will lead it to its fulfilment.'

This then is what I have to say to you. The name of your society is 'Society for the Protection of Religion'. Well, the protection of the religion, the protection and upraising before the world of the Hindu religion, that is the work before us. But what is the Hindu religion ? What is this religion which we call Sanatan, eternal ? It is the Hindu religion only because the Hindu nation has kept it, because in this Peninsula it grew up in the seclusion of the sea and the Himalayas, because in this sacred and ancient land it was given as a charge to the Aryan race to preserve through the ages. But it is not circumscribed by the confines of a single country, it does not belong peculiarly and for ever to a bounded part of the world. That which we call the Hindu religion is really the eternal religion, because it is the universal religion which embraces all others. If a religion is not universal, it cannot be eternal. A narrow religion, a sectarian religion, an exclusive religion can live only for a limited time and a limited purpose. This is the one religion that can triumph over materialism by including and anticipating the discoveries of science and the speculations of philosophy. It is the one religion which impresses on mankind the closeness of God to us and embraces in its compass all the possible means by which man can approach God. It is the one religion which insists every moment on the truth which all religions acknowledge that He is in all men and all things and that in Him we move and have our being. It is the one religion which enables us not only to understand and believe this truth but to realise it with every part of our being. It is the one religion which shows the world what the world is, that it is the Lila of Vasudeva. It is the one religion which shows us how we can best play our part in that Lila, its subtlest laws and its noblest rules. It is the one religion which does not separate life in any smallest detail from religion, which knows what immortality is and has utterly removed from us the reality of death.

This is the word that has been put into my mouth to speak to you today. What I intended to speak has been put away from me, and beyond what is given to me I have nothing to say. It is only the word that is put into me that I can speak to you. That word is now finished. I spoke once before with this force in me and I said then that this movement is not a political movement and that nationalism is not politics but a religion, a creed, a faith. I say it again today, but I put it in another way. I say no longer that nationalism is a creed, a religion, a faith; I say that it is the Sanatan Dharma which for us is nationalism. This Hindu nation was born with the Sanatan Dharma, with it it moves and with it it grows. When the Sanatan Dharma declines, then the nation declines, and if the Sanatan Dharma were capable of perishing, with the Sanatan Dharma it would perish.

The Sanatan Dharma, that is nationalism.

This is the message that I have to speak to you.

Appendix II

Sri Aurobindo wrote a message at the request of All India Radio, Tiruchirapalli, for broadcast on the eve of India's independence. As the text was too long, Sri Aurobindo revised and shortened it. The following is the text as broadcast.

August 15th, 1947 is the birthday of free India. It marks for her the end of an old era, the beginning of a new age. But we can also make it by our life and acts as a free nation an important date in a new age opening for the whole world, for the political, social, cultural and spiritual future of humanity.

August 15th is my own birthday and it is naturally gratifying to me that it should have assumed this vast significance. I take this coincidence, not as a fortuitous accident, but as the sanction and seal of the Divine Force that guides my steps on the work with which I began life, the beginning of its full fruition. Indeed, on this day I can watch almost all the world-movements which I hoped to see fulfilled in my lifetime, though then they looked like impracticable dreams, arriving at fruition or on their way to achievement. In all these movements free India may well play a large part and take a leading position.

The first of these dreams was a revolutionary movement which would create a free and united India. India today is free but she has not achieved unity. At one moment it almost seemed as if in the very act of liberation she would fall back into the chaos of separate States which preceded the British conquest.

But fortunately it now seems probable that this danger will be averted and a large and powerful, though not yet a complete union will be established. Also, the wisely drastic policy of the Constituent Assembly has made it probable that the problem of the depressed classes will be solved without schism or fissure. But the old communal division into Hindus and Muslims seems now to have hardened into a permanent political division of the country. It is to be hoped that this settled fact will not be accepted as settled for ever or as anything more than a temporary expedient. For if it lasts, India may be seriously weakened, even crippled: civil strife may remain always possible, possible even a new invasion and foreign conquest. India's internal development and prosperity may be impeded, her position among the nations weakened, her destiny impaired or even frustrated. This must not be; the partition must go. Let us hope that that may come about naturally, by an increasing recognition of the necessity not only of peace and concord but of common action, by the practice of common action and the creation of means for that purpose. In this way unity may finally come about under whatever form— the exact form may have a pragmatic but not a fundamental importance. But by whatever means, in whatever way, the division must go; unity must and will be achieved, for it is necessary for the greatness of India's future.

Another dream was for the resurgence and liberation of the peoples of Asia and her return to her great role in the progress of human civilisation. Asia has arisen; large parts are now quite free or are at this moment being liberated: its other still subject or partly subject parts are moving through whatever struggles towards freedom. Only a little has to be done and that will be done today or tomorrow. There India has her part to play and has begun to play it with an energy and ability which already indicate the measure of her possibilities and the place she can take in the council of the nations.

The third dream was a world-union forming the outer basis of a fairer, brighter and nobler life for all mankind. That unification of the human world is under way; there is an imperfect initiation organised but struggling against tremendous difficulties. But the momentum is there and it must inevitably increase and conquer. Here too India has begun to play a prominent part and, if she can develop that larger statesmanship which is not limited by the present facts and immediate possibilities but looks into the future and brings it nearer, her presence may make all the difference between a slow and timid and a bold and swift development. A catastrophe may intervene and interrupt or destroy what is being done, but even then the final result is sure. For unification is a necessity of Nature, an inevitable movement. Its necessity for the nations is also clear, for without it the freedom of the small nations may be at any moment in peril and the life even of the large and powerful nations insecure. The unification is therefore to the interests of all, and only human imbecility and stupid selfishness can prevent it; but these cannot stand for ever against the necessity of Nature and the Divine Will. But an outward basis is not enough; there must grow up an international spirit and outlook, international forms and institutions must appear, perhaps such developments as dual or multilateral citizenship, willed interchange or voluntary fusion of cultures. Nationalism will have fulfilled itself and lost its militancy and would no longer find these things incompatible with self-preservation and the integrality of its outlook. A new spirit of oneness will take hold of the human race.

Another dream, the spiritual gift of India to the world has already begun. India's spirituality is entering Europe and America in an ever increasing measure. That movement will grow; amid the disasters of the time more and more eyes are turning towards her with hope and there is even an increasing resort not only to her teachings, but to her psychic and spiritual practice.

The final dream was a step in evolution which would raise man to a higher and larger consciousness and begin the solution of the problems which have perplexed and vexed him since he first began to think and to dream of individual perfection and a perfect society. This is still a personal hope and an idea, an ideal which has begun to take hold both in India and in the West on forward-looking minds. The difficulties in the way are more formidable than in any other field of endeavour, but difficulties were made to be overcome and if the Supreme Will is there, they will be overcome. Here too, if this evolution is to take place, since it must proceed through a growth of the spirit and the inner consciousness, the initiative can come from India and, although the scope must be universal, the central movement may be hers.

Such is the content which I put into this date of India's liberation; whether or how far this hope will be justified depends upon the new and free India.

Appendix III

A message to America. The text was written for a celebration of Sri Aurobindo's 77th birthday in New York.

have been asked to send on this occasion of the fifteenth of August a message to the West, but what I have to say might be delivered equally as a message to the East. It has been customary to dwell on the division and difference between these two sections of the human family and even oppose them to each other; but, for myself I would rather be disposed to dwell on oneness and unity than on division and difference. East and West have the same human nature, a common human destiny, the same aspiration after a greater perfection, the same seeking after something higher than itself, something towards which inwardly and even outwardly we move. There has been a tendency in some minds to dwell on the spirituality or mysticism of the East and the materialism of the West; but the West has had no less than the East its spiritual seekings and, though not in profusion, its saints and sages and mystics, the East has had its materialistic tendencies, its material splendours, its similar or identical dealings with life and Matter and the world in which we live. East and West have always powerfully influenced each other and at the present day are under an increasing compulsion of Nature and Fate to do so more than ever before.

There is a common hope, a common destiny, both spiritual and material, for which both are needed as co-workers. It is no longer towards division and difference that we should turn our minds, but on unity, union, even oneness necessary for the pursuit and realization of a common ideal, the destined goal, the fulfilment towards which Nature in her beginning obscurely set out and must in an increasing light of knowledge replacing her first ignorance constantly persevere.

But what shall be that ideal and that goal? That depends on our conception of the realities of life and the supreme Reality.

Here we have to take into account that there has been, not any absolute difference but an increasing divergence between the tendencies of the East and the West. The highest truth is truth of the Spirit; a Spirit supreme above the world and yet immanent in the world and all that exists, sustaining and leading all towards whatever is the aim and goal and the fulfillment of Nature since her obscure inconscient beginnings through the growth of consciousness is the one aspect of existence which gives a clue to the secret of our being and a meaning to the world. The East has always and increasingly put the highest emphasis on the supreme truth of the Spirit; it has, even in its extreme philosophies, put the world away as an illusion and regarded the Spirit as the sole reality. The West has concentrated more and more increasingly on the world, on the dealings of mind and life with our material existence, on our mastery over it, on the perfection of mind and life and some fulfillment of the human being here: latterly this has gone so far as the denial of the Spirit and even the enthronement of Matter as the sole reality. Spiritual perfection as the sole ideal on one side, on the other, the perfectibility of the race, the perfect society, a perfect development of the human mind and life and man's material existence have become the largest dream of the future. Yet both are truths and can be regarded as part of the Spirit in world-nature; they are not incompatible with each other: rather their divergence has to be healed and both have to be included and reconciled in our view of the future.

The Science of the West has discovered evolution as the secret of life and its process in this material world; but it has laid more stress on the growth of form and species than on the growth of consciousness: even, consciousness has been regarded as an incident and not the whole secret of the meaning of the evolution. An evolution has been admitted by certain minds in the East, certain philosophies and Scriptures, but there its sense has been the growth of the soul through developing or successive forms and many lives of the individual to its own higher reality. For if there is a conscious being in the form, that being can hardly be a temporary phenomenon of consciousness; it must be a soul fulfilling itself and this fulfillment can only take place if there is a return of the sould to earth in many successive lives, in many successive bodies.

The process of evolution has been the development from and inconscient Matter of a subconscient and then a conscious Life, of conscious mind first in animal life and then fully in conscious and thinking man, the highest present achievement in evolutionary Nature. The achievement of mental being is at present her highest and tends to be regarded as her final work; butb it is possible to conceive a still further step of the evolution: Nature may have in view beyond the imperfect mind of man a consciousness that passes out of the mind's ignorance and possesses truth as its inherent right and nature. There is a truth-consciousness as it is called in the Veda, a supermind, as I have termed it, possessing Knowledge, not having to seek after it and constantly miss it. In one of the Upanishads a being of knowledge is stated to be the next step above the mental being; into that the soul has to rise and through it to attain the perfect bliss of spiritual existence. If that could be achieved as the next evolutionary step of Nature here, then she would be fulfilled and we could conceive of the perfection of life even here, its attainment of a full spiritual living even in this body or it may be in a perfected body. We could even speak of a divine life on earth; our human dream of perfectibility would be accomplished and at the same time the aspiration to a heaven on earth common to several religions and spiritual seers and thinkers.

The ascent of the human soul to the supreme Spirit is that soul's highest aim and necessity, for that is the supreme reality; but there can be too the descent of the Spirit and its powers into the world and that would justify the existence of the material world also, give a meaning, a divine purpose to the creation and solve its riddle. East and West could be reconciled in the pursuit of the highest and largest ideal, Spirit embrace Matter and Matter find its own true reality and hidden Reality in all things in the Spirit.

11-8-49 Sri Aurobindo

Bibliography

Argov, Daniel, *Moderates and Extremists in the Indian Nationalist Movement, 1883–1910*, Asia Publishing House, 1967.

Banerjee, Aparna, *Integral Philosophy of Sri Aurobindo*, Centre for Sri Aurobindo Studies, Jadavpur University, in Association with Decent Books, 2012.

Banerjee, Anurag (ed.), *Sri Aurobindo and His Essential Thoughts*, Overman Foundation, 2015.

—— (ed.), *Sri Aurobindo: His Political Life and Activities*, Overman Foundation, 2012.

—— (ed.), *Sri Aurobindo and Rabindranath Tagore*, Overman Foundation, 2011.

Banerji, Debashish, *Seven Quartets of Becoming: A Transformational Yoga Psychology : Based on the Diaries of Sri Aurobindo*, Nalanda International and DK Printworld, 2012.

Basu, Samar, *Glimpses of Vedantism in Sri Aurobindo's Political Thought*, Sri Mira Trust, 1998.

Bhattacharya, Sabyasachi, *Talking Back: The Idea of Civilization in the Indian Nationalist Discourse*, OUP India, 2011.

Chattopadhyaya, D.P., *Sri Aurobindo on Man*, Sri Aurobindo Pathmandir, 1972.

Chelysheva, Irina, *Ethical Ideas in the World Outlook of Swami Vivekananda, Lokmanya BG Tilak and Aurobindo Ghose*, Vostok, 1989.

Giri, Ananta Kumar (ed.), *Mahatma Gandhi and Sri Aurobindo*, Routledge India, 2021.

Dalton, Dennis, *Indian Idea of Freedom: Political Thought of Swami Vivekananda, Aurobindo Ghose, Rabindranath Tagore and Mahatma Gandhi*, The Academic Press, 1982.

Das, Bijoy Prasad (ed), *Sri Aurobindo's Philosophy of Nationalism*, Avenel Press, 2017.

Das, Manoj, *Sri Aurobindo: Life and Times of the Mahayogi* (The Pre-Pondicherry Phase), Sri Aurobindo International Centre of Education, 2020.

——, *Sri Aurobindo in the First Decade of the 20th Century*, Sri Aurobindo Ashram, 2003.

Das, M.N., *India Under Minto and Morley: Politics Behind Revolution, Repression and Reforms*, G. Allen and Unwin, 1964.

Das, Swarnmala, *Sri Aurobindo: A Modern Political Thinker*, Ajanta, 1993.

Diwakar, R.R., *Mahayogi: Life, Sadhana and Teachings of Sri Aurobindo*, Bharatiya Vidya Bhawan, 1999.

Dutta, Madhumita, *Sri Aurobindo: A Legend*, Avenel Press, 2016.

Gandhi, Kishor, *Social Philosophy of Sri Aurobindo and the New Age*, Sri Aurobindo Ashram, 1991.

Ganguly, Anirban, *Debating Culture*, DK Printworld, 2013.

Ghosh, Barindra Kumar, *The Tale of My Exile: Twelve Years in the Andamans*, Sri Aurobindo Ashram, 2011.

——, *Meri Atmakhatha* (My autobiography in Hindi), Ashir Prakashan, 2011.

——, *The Truth of Life*, S Ganesan, 1922.

Ghose, Barin, *Sri Aurobindo as I Knew Him*, unpublished manuscript.

Ghose, J.C., *Life-Work of Sri Aurobindo*, Atmashakti Library, 1929.

Goyal, O.P., *Studies in Modern Indian Political Thought: The Moderates and the Extremists*, Kitab Mahal, 1964.

Guha, Arun Chandra, *Aurobindo and Jugantar*, Sahitya Samsad.

Hartz, Richard, *The Clasp of Civilizations: Globalization and Religion in a Multicultural World*, D.K. Printworld, 2015.

Heehs, Peter (ed.), *Situating Sri Aurobindo; A Reader*, OUP, 2013.

——, *The Lives of Sri Aurobindo*, Columbia University Press, 2008.

——, *Nationalism, Religion, and Beyond: Writings on Politics, Society and Culture by Sri Aurobindo*, OUP, 2005.

——, *Nationalism, Terrorism, Communalism: Essays in Indian History*, OUP, 1998.

—— (ed.), *The Essential Writings of Sri Aurobindo*, OUP, 1998.

———, *Sri Aurobindo: A Brief Biography*, OUP, 1989.

———, *India's Freedom Struggle 1857–1947: A Short History*, OUP, 1988.

Hiranmayi, *Sri Aurobindo in Surat*, Sri Aurobindo Society, Surat, 2007.

Huchzermeyer, Wilfried, *Sri Aurobindo's Commentaries on Krishna, Buddha, Christ and Ramakrishna: Their Role in the Evolution of Humanity*, edition sawitri, 2018.

———, *Sri Aurobindo and European Philosophy*, Prisma, 2016.

———, *Sri Aurobindo: Saga of a Great Indian Sage*, D.K. Printworld, 2013.

Iyengar, K.R. Srinivasa, *On The Mother: The Chronicle of a Manifestation and a Ministry*, Sri Aurobindo International Centre of Education, 1994.

———, *Sri Aurobindo: A Biography and a History*, Sri Aurobindo International Centre of Education, 1972.

Kanungo, Hem Chandra, and Amiya Samanta (ed.), *Account of the Revolutionary Movement in Bengal*, Setu Prakashani, 2015.

Ker, James Campbell, *Political Trouble in India, 1907–17*, Mahadevprasad Saha (ed.), Editions India, 1973.

Keshavmurti, *Sri Aurobindo: The Hope of Man*, Dipti Publications, 1969.

Mahapatra, Debidatta Aurobinda, *The Philosophy of Sri Aurobindo: Indian Philosophy and Yoga in the Contemporary World*, Bloomsbury, 2020.

McDermott, Robert (ed.), *Six Pillars: Introductions to the Major Works of Sri Aurobindo*, Wilson Books, 1974.

Mitra, Sisirkumar, *The Quest for Divine Consciousness*, India Book Company, 1972.

———, *The Liberator: Sri Aurobindo: India and the world*, Jaico, 1954.

Mundschenk, Paul Ernest, *Up from Belittlement: Sri Aurobindo and the Response to British Colonialism in India*, unpublished PhD thesis, Claremont Graduate School, 1976.

Minor, Robert Neil (ed.), *Modern Indian Interpreters of the Bhagvad Gita*, Suny Series in Religious Studies, 1986.

———, *Sri Aurobindo: The Perfect and the Good*, Minerva, 1978.

Mohanty, Sachidananda, *Cosmopolitan Modernity in Early 20th-Century India*, Routledge, 2015.

Nandakumar, Prema, *Sister Nivedita and Sri Aurobindo*, Sri Ramakrishna Math, 2017.

Navajata, *Sri Aurobindo*, National Book Trust, 1972.

Nahar, Sujata, *Mother's Chronicles Book Six: Mirra In South India*, Mira Aditi Centre, 2001.

——, *Mother's Chronicles Book Five: Mirra Meets the Revolutionary*, Mira Aditi Centre, 1997.

——, *Mother's Chronicles Book Four: Mirra—Sri Aurobindo*, Mira Aditi Centre, 1995.

——, *Mother's Chronicles Book Three: Mirra the Occultist*, Mira Aditi Centre, 1989.

——, *Mother's Chronicles Book Two: Mirra the Artist*, Mira Aditi Centre, 1986.

——, *Mother's Chronicles Book One: Mirra*, Mira Aditi Centre, 1985.

O'Connor, June, *The Quest for Political and Spiritual Liberation: A Study in the Thought of Sri Aurobindo Ghose*, Associated University Presses, 1977.

Orton, Martha S.G., *Journey to Oneness*, SACAR, 2011.

Panda, Sunayana, *Sri Aurobindo and the Cripps Mission*, First Feature, 2012.

Pandit, M.P., *Sri Aurobindo*, Publications Division, Ministry of Information and Broadcasting , Govt. of India, 1983.

Pantham, Thomas, and Kenneth L. Deutsch, *Political Thought in Modern India*, Sage, 1986.

Pearson, Nathaniel, *Sri Aurobindo and the Soul Quest of Man*, G. Allen and Unwin, 1952.

Price, Joan, *An Introduction to Sri Aurobindo's Philosophy*, Sri Aurobindo Ashram, 1977.

Purani, A.B., *Evening Talks with Sri Aurobindo*, Sri Aurobindo Ashram, 2007.

——, *The Life of Sri Aurobindo*, Sri Aurobindo Ashram, 1978.

Ranchan, Som P., and K.D. Gupta, *Sri Aurobindo As a Political Thinker: An Interdisciplinary Study*, Konark Publisher, 1988.

Rao, T. Kodandarama, *At the Feet of the Master*, Sri Aurobindo Ashram, 1969.

Ray, Trija, *Sri Aurobindo and Uttarpara Speech*, Uttarpara Sri Aurobindo Parishad, 2017.

——, *Sri Aurobindo and The Hooghly Conference*, Sri Aurobindo Bhavan Hooghly Chuchura, 2014.

Reddy, Ananda, and Sachidananda Mohanty, *Essentials of Sri Aurobindo's Thought*, Institute of Human Study, 1997.

Reddy, Ananda, *Four Aspects of Savitri*, Sri Aurobindo Centre for Advanced Research, 2016.

Rishabhchand, *Sri Aurobindo: His Life Unique*, Sri Aurobindo Ashram, 1981.

Roarke, Jesse, *Sri Aurobindo*, Sri Aurobindo Ashram Press, 1973.

Roshan and Apurva (eds), *Sri Aurobindo in Baroda*, Sri Aurobindo Ashram Publications Division, 1993.

Roy, Dinendra Kumar, *With Aurobindo in Baroda*, Sri Aurobindo Ashram, 2006.

Roy, Niharendu, *Alipore Conspiracy Case*, New House, 2016.

Sanyal, Indrani, and Krishna Roy (eds), *Sri Aurobindo and His Contemporary Thinkers*, DK Printworld/Jadavpur University, 2007.

Sanyal, Indrani and Krishna Roy, *Understanding Thoughts of Sri Aurobindo*, DK Printworld/Jadavpur University, 2007.

Sarma, G.N. (ed.), *Sri Aurobindo and The Indian Renaissance*, Ultra Publications, 1997.

——, *The Vision of Sri Aurobindo*, Dipti, 1973.

Sarkar, Sunit, *The Swadeshi Movement in Bengal, 1903–1908*, People's Publishing House, 1973.

Seidlitz, Larry, *Transforming Lives: An introduction to Sri Aurobindo's Integral Yoga*, Sri Aurobindo Centre for Advanced Research, 2014.

Sethna, K.D., *The Vision and Work of Sri Aurobindo*, Mother India, 1968.

Singh, Karan, *Prophet of Indian Nationalism: A Study of the Political Thought of Sri Aurobindo Ghosh 1893–1910*, G. Allen and Unwin, 1963.

Sharma, Ram Nath, *The Philosophy of Sri Aurobindo*, Kedar Nath Ram Nath, 1977.

Sri Aurobindo, *Bengali Writings*, Sri Aurobindo Ashram, 1997.

Sri Aurobindo, *Bhawani Bharathi*, Sri Aurobindo Society, 2003.

Sri Aurobindo, *Sri Aurobindo Birth Centenary Library*, Vols 1–30, Sri Aurobindo Ashram, 1970–73.

Sri Aurobindo, *Tales of Prison Life*, Sri Aurobindo Ashram, 1974.

Sri Aurobindo, *The Collected Works of Sri Aurobindo*, Vols 1–37, Sri Aurobindo Ashram, 1997.

Tripathy, Sabita, and Nanda Kishore Mishra, *Tracts for His Times: Bande*

Mataram and Sri Aurobindo's Anti-Colonial Discourse, Authors Press, 2016.

Varma, V.P., *The Political Philosophy of Sri Aurobindo*, Motilal Banrasidas, 1976.

Venet, Luc, *Sri Aurobindo and The Revolution of India*, Createspace Independent Pub, 2017.

Wolpert, Stanley A., *Morley and India 1906–1910*, University of California Press, 1967.

www.ingramcontent.com/pod-product-compliance
Lightning Source LLC
Chambersburg PA
CBHW032215071025
33724CB00033B/951